POPULISM

MICHAEL BURLEIGH

Populism

Before and After the Pandemic

HURST & COMPANY, LONDON

THE ENGELSBERG LECTURES,
LSE IDEAS, 2019–20

First published in the United Kingdom in 2021 by
C. Hurst & Co. (Publishers) Ltd.,
41 Great Russell Street, London, WC1B 3PL
© Michael Burleigh, 2021
All rights reserved.
Printed in Great Britain by Bell and Bain Ltd, Glasgow

Distributed in the United States, Canada and Latin America
by Oxford University Press, 198 Madison Avenue,
New York, NY 10016, United States of America.

The right of Michael Burleigh to be identified as the author
of this publication is asserted by him in accordance with
the Copyright, Designs and Patents Act, 1988.

A Cataloguing-in-Publication data record for this book
is available from the British Library.

ISBN: 9781787384682

This book is printed using paper from registered sustainable
and managed sources.

www.hurstpublishers.com

CONTENTS

WE THE PEOPLE

The last time I lectured at the LSE, in the early 1990s, my talk was probably about the Nazis, by then a niche preoccupation in a world mesmerised by the end of the Cold War in Europe. Imagine my surprise to find that nowadays the Führer's face is ubiquitous; in fact there is even a history of his face. I haven't read it. We all also know the television history channels which should be renamed Hitler channels, where the last global war is on a continuous loop.

Many of you will have read new books dedicated to the expiry of democracy, or the problems it is encountering in late middle age.

There is also a newfound and urgent interest in the imminence of tyranny. The historian Timothy Snyder had success with a civics primer designed to help identify signs of creeping tyranny in the era of President Trump.

The literary historian Stephen Greenblatt contributed *Shakespeare on Power*, which alludes to the then president on every page, without ever mentioning him. Critics joked that Greenblatt has a bad case of the 'DTs', seeing Trump rather than creepy crawlies on the ceiling. This last book had a lot of powerful admirers. The holidaying Chancellor Merkel was photographed reading Greenblatt, in preference to the avalanche of new social science books on populism. Good for her.

Liberal warnings about the recrudescence of fascism and tyranny have no monopoly on lessons from the past. Among European populists, to range no further, mythologised or *weaponised* history abounds. It often consists of post-modernist mash-ups, worthy of the disturbing content one can see on Russian television every night.

A recent video showed Spain's far-right VOX party leader Santiago Abascal on a horse, re-enacting the medieval Reconquista, to the theme music of 'Lord of the Rings'. His party had just doubled its number of seats in parliament at a time of renewed crisis with the Catalan nationalists. Bang goes the belief in Iberian exceptionalism. An Alternative für Deutschland election poster used Gérôme's nineteenth-century Orientalist painting of a 'Slave Market' to ensure that 'Europe does not become Eurabia'.

Then there is this sceptre'd isle, as Shakespeare put it. With the Brexit party using air raid sirens and searchlights to announce Mr Farage, I am often confused whether we are living in the 'Darkest Hour' of 1940; or, as some suggest, the early modern Civil War without swords and muskets. Or a re-run of the Protestant Reformation as we once more break with Brussels and (the Treaty of) Rome. This last bizarre conceit is especially popular among the conservative Roman Catholics who own and write for the Brexity *Daily Telegraph* which used to be a respectable newspaper.

Right now I want to escape the dreary gravity of Hitler, not least because the EU's twenty-seven nations have their own distinctive histories which we should respect. History is supposed to broaden the mind, not restrict our collective imaginations to the Nazis. But first I must optimistically rehearse why our time is unlike the interwar era.

Our European present has not just emerged from a global war that killed eighteen million people and which destroyed four major empires by its episodic conclusion in 1918–22, though something resembling the Spanish flu pandemic is stalking us.

We have experienced nothing comparable to the political effects of the hyper-inflation and Depression which book-ended the Weimar Republic's tragic history, and in the case of inflation destroyed the middle class, their money and liberal political parties.

Our streets are not overrun by uniformed paramilitaries assaulting and murdering their rivals often with the complicity of policemen and courts, though there has been an uptick in the incidence of assassinations of democratic politicians from Jo Cox to Walter Lübcke, both killed by neo-Nazis.

Most contemporary European societies are strikingly demilitarised, as the Stanford historian James Sheehan showed in a rather good book, even though European defence spending is three times that of Russia, some of it for export. Nowhere in Europe are the military out of civilian control, as was the case of the political generals

3

of Weimar, or the imperialistic Japanese ones who from 1932–45 hijacked the government. The retired three-star German air force general who is an AfD mayoral candidate seems eccentric.

Hardly anyone other than the evil or insane regards violence as essential to the birth of a new Fascist type of being, let alone the idea that national salvation *will* (not *might*) result from exterminating entire races. As David Runciman says, wars of national survival discredited far right politics for a couple of generations; since we are unlikely to have one, there is not going to be such a drastic resolution to populism. The incompetence of braggart demagogues in major crises may however be their undoing. Fomenting social division, promoting polarisation, scorning professional expertise, cowing civil servants, and above all acting as advocates for the most ignorant and uneducated elements in our societies, does not work when—for example—a killer virus is working its way through every nation.

This is not to recommend complacency towards that era of religoid totalitarianism, to whose exploration I devoted two decades of my writing life.

It is crucial to be alert to worrying affinities. One cannot read Sebastian Hafner's *Defying Hitler* without noting the implosion of the moderate political centre, which is happening nowadays particularly in the case of European Social Democracy. The re-emergence of movement politics, within or outside political parties, is also disturbing, most obviously in the case of PEGIDA, the German acronym for Patriotic Europeans Against the Islamisation of the Occident which from October 2014 onwards marched in East German cities.

There is depressing relevancy in what the Viennese satirist Karl Kraus, the English novelist George Orwell, or German philologist Victor Klemperer noted about the creeping brutalisation of thought and language and the temptation of the tribal tom-tom beat, as Orwell called it.

Nor should we forget the exiled German Catholic historian Eric Voegelin's contempt for a conservative 'elite rabble' which was disastrously porous towards the Hitlerites. He meant Papen, Schleicher and all the other posh vons.

There is much culpable porosity around nowadays, as well as transgressive speech which helps lower the threshold to violence, most disturbingly visible inside the US Capitol on 6 January 2021. In various countries, there is also a Jacobin-style mobocracy, only some of it confined to online platforms. Britain is not alone either in having politicised hooligans. The German equivalent to Stephen Yaxley-Lennon, aka Tommy Robinson, founder of the English Defence League, is a convicted burglar and drug-dealer called Lutz Bachmann who founded PEGIDA.

But before moving to a more recent past I think needs attention, I want to rehearse some thoughts about populism for those who might not be as familiar with this subject as historians or political scientists.

By populism I mean the identification of the people as an organic and uniquely virtuous whole, ignored or malignly divided by corrupt and oligarchic elites.

Populism restores the illusion of efficacy to those who feel their views are ignored by identikit managerial politicians, while constitutional checks and balances actively frustrate the translation of the people's will into policy through elected delegates. Mr Dominic Cummings's 2016 slogan 'take back control' actually captures the sense of regaining agency rather well, though it is likely to prove entirely illusory.

This goes with a kind of moral indignancy, more usually characteristic of the Left, on the part of a majoritarian Right which has appropriated the grievance culture of minority identity politics.

Arlie Hochschild's *Strangers in Their Own Land* is a fine account of how that has played out in the US, especially in her metaphor of people becoming impatient with waiting in line for rewards that never come, while others cut in ahead of them.

A similar sense of victimhood is pervasive across the European populist right. Rarely can we have heard so much from people who claim to be voiceless, yet who are protected from scorn by a kind of right-wing political correctness. Actually, they have plenty of articulate ventriloquists too, many writing for magazines and websites which are the toys of hedgefund millionaires. For example the Brexit-supporting political philosopher John Gray blames liberal 'bien pensants' for this state of affairs, writing 'Populism is the creation of a liberal political class that blames its decline on the stupidity of voters'. The Brexit supporting academic Matthew Goodwin has never seen an extreme right party he could not find excuses for.

Many bewildered liberals may be silently assenting to something said by the great eighteenth-century French reactionary thinker Joseph de Maistre:

'The principle of the sovereignty of the people is so dangerous that, even if it were true, it would be necessary to conceal it'.

I know many liberals who feel like that, some of whom advocate an epistocracy in which voters are differentially weighed according to criteria like education.

Unlike major ideologies, there is no founding text which encapsulates populism, as there are for liberalism, Marxism or reaction.

That is why the Dutch scholar Cas Mudde calls populism a thin ideology bolstered with extraneous elements from other political traditions. That can lead to incoherence.

British populist ideologues and leaders, for example, are divided between demands for more spending by a state construed as the Wagnerian 'magic spear which heals all wounds', as the nineteenth-century Prussian historian and politician Friedrich Dahlmann called it. But others are animated by the happy vision of 'Singapore on Thames' which excites some hedge-fund bosses.

In reality this would leave everyone outside the M-25 motorway in a colder Malaya without the rubber and tin, including most supporters of Brexit who on every projection are going to take the largest economic hit from the strategy they enthusiastically support as if it were a kind of religious faith.

One can further define populism as a supposedly 'authentic' rhetorical style, in which shameless lies are part of the charm; as a series of family resemblances akin to the Habsburg jaw in portraiture; or as a shadowy near-relation to democracy that in times of turmoil looms over the object.

Maybe these definitions are too bland, for in all cases, conspiracy theories are involved, namely the belief that 'liberal' global and national elites are actively conniving to thwart the righteous will of the people because they fundamentally despise them. Remember the old joke that Tony Blair so hated the English working class that he sought out a less inert Polish one to replace them. It ceased to be a joke some time ago.

Recall too prime minister Gordon Brown dismissing a 'bigoted woman' during the 2010 election on a microphone that was still live, or Hillary Clinton's remark, six years later, about half of Trump's supporters belonging in a 'basket of deplorables'—by which she meant, further excavating her own grave, 'They're racist, sexist, homophobic, xenophobic—Islamophobic—you name it'.

What claims to be holistic is in fact highly divisive, and involves many of us being rendered 'unreal'.

Populism involves a sleight of hand in which the People must be sub-divided into the authentically real ones, who intuit what is right, and the cosmopolitan unrooted who could be everywhere and nowhere, as prime minister Theresa May notoriously put it, echoing the British journalist David Goodhart.

'*Vox populi, vox Dei*' as Mr Mogg puts it with his usual condescending smirk. Actually the cliche of 'ordinary people' is highly constructed, though we accept vox pops all the time. It derives from the Second World War and films like 1945's *Brief Encounter* in which Celia Johnson protests: 'I am just an ordinary woman'. Ordinary people were celebrated as the common-sense alternative to academics, bureaucrats and experts.

Unlike inter-war fascists, most populists are not anti-democratic. They can't get enough of voting. Italy's Five Star Movement would have us all voting online 24/7, a truly nightmarish prospect and one which would lend itself to obsessives—to be charitable. Imagine all the online poker addicts switching late at night to put side bets on the outcome of referenda and trying to alter the results.

There is also what Mudde and others call 'the democratisation of democracy' which is harder to controvert. One effect of populism, whether in Latin America, Britain or Germany, has been to revitalise democracy, in the first case by empowering indigenous peoples excluded by Hispanic elites, in the second and third by coaxing lifelong non-voters to the ballots, often meaning voting AfD or Brexit Party. It is hard to deplore political apathy and then object when people vote in record numbers, though as many argue voting is only the half of it, for people vote in Russia and Turkey too.

These core beliefs of populism have been around a long time. As an historian I'd better include some more history.

Just recall the idealistic peasant-worshipping *Narodnik* students of Tsarist Russia, who like anthropologists discovered their own peasantry rather than a new tribe of hunter-gatherers in Siberia. Many were so appalled by their lack of resonance among these God- and Tsar-fearing folk that they took to terrorism instead.

Or there is the *Wizard of Oz* world of American Democrat demagogue William Jennings Bryan. Both the 1900 book and the 1939 film are an allegory of populism in which Oz is short for ounce of gold or silver and the failed demagogue Bryan himself is the lion without a roar. The wicked witches of the compass are Eastern bankers and railroad barons. There was a nasty anti-Chinese racism too.

Such a brief history would encompass such evanescent figures as Guglielmo Giannini and Pierre Poujade in post-war France and Italy. The latter launched the political career of an equally antisemitic 27-year-old soldier called Jean Marie Le Pen, who in 1956 was elected a Poujadist deputy, the youngest in the Assembly, before resuming a military career in Algeria as a professional torturer of Arabs and going on to lead the Front National.

Poujade and Giannini remained what seemed to be backwards-facing figures because the main ideological conflict was the Cold War struggle between the partisans of liberal democracy and Soviet Communism, rather than about newsagents, parfumiers or tobacconists being wiped out by department stores and supermarkets and extortionate taxes. The milk-drinking prime minister Pierre Mendès-France, who was Jewish, excited special hatreds in a nation of vin rouge and Pernod lovers.

The rise of populist parties has been more gradual and fissiparous than people without historical memory assume.

Of the fifty-five most successful parties, twenty-eight were founded before 2000, and only sixteen after the turn of the millennium. Perhaps the end of bipolar superpower conflict had something to do with the latter?

Certainly many populists regard President Vladimir Putin as a kind of national sovereigntist hero, battling against what he calls 'Gayropa'. Indeed, the fusion of chauvinism, religoid social conservativism and pro-babies welfarism of Hungary's Fidesz or Poland's Law and Justice party are almost identical to that of Putin's own United Russia party, albeit without the great power pretensions. Of all the populist formulae, that is proba-bly the one with the most traction.

The most venerable populist parties include the Austrian Freedom Party, established in 1956; Ulster's DUP and the Swiss People's Party, both founded in 1971; and France's Front National which was formed a year later.

You are mostly too young to remember the advent of the DUP, but they were the abrasive voice of the East Belfast Protestant working class. Their voluble Free Presbyterian leader Ian Paisley sounded very different from the Captains this, or Major thats—meaning war veteran posh landowners—who had dominated Ulster Unionism.

Nowadays populist parties are part of every third European government, with two in sole power (Hungary and Poland), and half a dozen in ruling coalitions. According to the authoritative Swedish Timbro index for 2018, such parties are supported by roughly a quar-ter of European voters. To adopt a football metaphor, many have expanded beyond the early hooligans to the regular family fans.

The reasons why national populism has erupted in the last decade are not especially mysterious, though it is not the ineluctable movement that its academic boosters imagine.

Greece recently reverted to a classic two-party system, except with the defeated Syriza replacing Pasok on the left, and not a single seat for the neo-nazi Golden Dawn. The latter then shut down its Athens headquarters after a dismal 2.9% share of the vote amidst a conservative landslide. The most recent Austrian election saw the Freedom Party vote fall from 26% in 2017 to 16.2%, admittedly in the wake of a bizarre corruption scandal on Ibiza involving their leader. In Slovakia the populist Smer-DS were ousted by a party called 'Ordinary People and Independent Personalities', while the Romanians preferred a president whose slogan was 'Make Romania a Normal Country Again'.

In Hungary the all-triumphal Fidesz, a party dedicated to Christian family values you will recall, lost control of eleven of the country's twenty-three major towns this autumn, not least because one of their mayoral candidates used public money to fund cocaine fuelled orgies on a yacht off Croatia. He was re-elected as it happens, for life moves in strange ways, but his antics damaged his colleagues.

The Netherlands have often been cited as another hotbed of populism, symbolised by the bleach-blonde Geert Wilders. But his shock value has worn off, and he had competition from Thierry Baudet, a smart yuppy who speaks Latin as fluently as the pope.

Baudet's Forum for Democracy party had some success as a novelty, until the antisemitism of its leaders became very public. But he repelled many with allusions to a 'Boreal civilisation'—meaning primordial white northern forest dwellers apparently. A climate change denier who believes women want to be dominated, here is Baudet rejoicing in electoral success:

> Like all the other countries in our boreal world we are being destroyed by the very people who are supposed to protect us. We are being undermined by our universities, our journalists. By people who get art subsidies and who design our buildings.

The longer history of populism reveals many party vehicles being tested and rejected.

Recall the Referendum Party, the Anti-Federalist League, Ukip—founded in the LSE history department—and Veritas in Britain, with Brexit Ltd as the latest vehicle. The AfD has split too, with the supposedly more moderate Frauke Petry decamping to form a new party called The Blues to hoover up bourgeois nationalists who don't want to rub shoulders with extremists like Björn Höcke, head of the AfD in Thuringia. His 'Wing' of the party is so extreme that Germany's domestic security service, the Bundesamt für Verfassungsschutz, has authorised agent infiltration and wiretaps against it, though Matthew Goodwin won't be racing to tell you that.

But these national populist parties simultaneously exert a gravitational pull on mainstream parties, transforming their terms of reference.

Worse, they can act as the human equivalent of aggressive African bees wiping out more placid indigenous hives, the fate of America's Republicans and Britain's Conservatives. This confronts politicians of a centrist disposition, whether British or German conservatives, with a difficult dilemma: leave or form coalitions, perhaps in order to defang the populists through enforced responsibility, which seems freighted with multiple dangers.

Nor have we witnessed a general Springtime of the nationalists as the British conservative minister Michael Gove enthused before Brexit led virtually all European Eurosceptics to regard the UK as an international basket-case.

Weak common denominators preclude concerted activity, for this is really not like Europe in 1848 with its galaxy of liberal national liberators hoping to free their nations from multinational empires. That is why contemporary populists have to caricature the EU as a Fourth Reich or EuSSR as if a freely entered association of states is an updated form of the militant totalitarianism the 1951 Coal and Steel Community was created to transcend.

Europe's populists have not had much success either in forging their own bloc in the European Parliament, where they are strewn between at least three rival groups because of ideological or personality clashes.

While supporters of the EU should rejoice that every single national populist party has abandoned emulating the British with Grexit, Italexit and so on, the bad news is that they are resolved to work inside the EU Parliament and institutions to bring about their colourful vision of confederated nation states which will pull the plug on elite liberalism. As in national parliaments, coalition-building will be difficult and protracted—imagine what Spain is undergoing.

We should also mention the external actors who do not wish the EU well either. One is President Putin who would like to divide the EU while detaching it from the US. He has close relations with Le Pen, Orban and Salvini, while using gas pipelines to foster discord between EU member states—Germany and Poland for example. Brexit is also a golden opportunity to take Anglo-Russian relations out of the freezer, and to exploit the former's impending apartness. His oligarch cyphers are busy corrupting the House of Lords and others, though we were not being allowed to read the report about this.

Former President Trump is no fan of the EU either, regarding the Europeans as a burden on the tax-paying Uncle Sucker, while Europe's farmers, aircraft- and auto-manufacturers benefit from state subsidies.

Meanwhile Trump's quondam advisor Steve Bannon, a subversive apocalyptic Catholic multi-millionaire, has been trying to coordinate European populist movements through what you might call a kind of Popintern resembling the Comintern in the 1930s—without much success, since many populists have a history of anti-Americanism, which is only partly mitigated by their enthusiasm for Trump. He is a law unto himself, as one saw when he favoured Italy's technocrat prime minister—Giuseppe 'great job' Conte—over his Italy First soulmate Matteo Salvini in 2019.

None of the above is to deny that populism speaks to real concerns. Something must be driving ordinary French people to spend their weekends camped on miserable rural roundabouts discussing issues like green fuel taxes or the negative impacts of the gig economy on their children's futures.

It seems to many that elites have much to answer for, though their cosmopolitanism is the least of it, as the LSE's Andrés Velasco has written in a spirited defence of it as something more than sipping cappuchinos at Davos among the global rich. It means being open to humanity as a whole—meaning languages, culture and so on—something our civilisation has prided itself on since the time of Herodotus. He was certainly patriotic about ancient Greek culture too.

Elites discredited themselves, whether through the lies told to legitimise the 2003 invasion of Iraq and then Libya in 2011, or serial corruption scandals—some in the 1990s—in Britain, France, Italy, Spain and Germany's Dieselgate emissions scandal.

Italy's 'clean hands' investigation in the 1990s swept up 251 MPs, four former prime ministers, five party leaders, and seven former cabinet ministers. Ten suspects killed themselves to avoid trial. At the time I was teaching a young Italian here who seemed permanently depressed. He was the son of a major RAI television executive. I asked what was wrong. 'Most of my father's friends are in jail' he replied.

Corruption combined with managerial professionalism to add substance to the idea that politicians were what comedian Beppe Grillo denounced as *la casta*. Politicophobia ensues: they are all the same, and all on the take and easily amenable to the corrosive effects of satire, which is rarely reverse-engineered towards the satirists.

One solution is to turn to ENSIDS, or 'empathetic non-self-interested decision makers'. That's a mouthful so I'll repeat it. It means the likes of the billionaires Ross Perot, Silvio Berlusconi and Donald Trump, or indeed to comedians and entertainers like Grillo. Ukraine elected one too. The problem is that they can be liars too, with Trump having told an estimated 20,000 of them since he came to office.

One should not underrate the appeal of rogues in societies where informal social norms have atrophied to embrace crooks and tax dodgers as well as litter, swearing, truancy and so on. Berlusconi not only said 'I am like you', but he also winked 'I can be as bad as anyone', something brilliantly portrayed in Paolo Sorrentino's movie *Loro (Them)*. Mr Trump took this to another level entirely with his crude jokes about grabbing women, avoiding taxes and how rich he is, allegedly.

Britain's publicity-addict prime minister Boris Johnson vaulted to national prominence, first by changing his *Times* byline from Alexander to the more evocative Boris and by writing lies about straight bananas and condoms for fishermen mandated by Brussels, but mainly as a mop-haired comedian on *Have I Got News for You*. Trump fired people on *The Apprentice*.

Incidentally, whereas working class people had much bitter experience of middle-class professionals who upbraided them for feeding their children fried chicken and for smoking or who queried their welfare claims, the billionaire class of personage had a glamorous lifestyle which they eagerly consumed under the hair-drier. Especially if the billionaire spoke their language too. By contrast, the class-obsessed British have always been suckers for articulate toffs, like Johnson or the absurd Mr Mogg, the Honorable Member for the eighteenth century.

This brings us to the matter of exclusion, or rather the extrusion of people from working class backgrounds from political life and its professionalisation as a career. The most striking thing about David Cameron's recent *Memoir* is its insider's description of the life of a typical quadrangle person, as I call them, moving along a conveyor belt from Eton and Balliol to the very top, with the aid of nepotism at every stage, until there is enough money for a decorous Gypsy caravan to write a memoir in.

In the case of Britain's Labour party, whereas in the 1920s 80 per cent of MPs had working class backgrounds, that is true of only 8 per cent today, while in France only 2 per cent of politicians so self-describe, despite Macron's attempts to open politics to what are tellingly called 'civilians' by the 'professionals'.

The effects of elite intermarriage and nepotism should be mentioned too, something even more glaringly apparent in the media, if one is alert to recurrent surnames. Fields like pop music, television and acting—where working class people once distinguished themselves—have also been colonised by the well-resourced—Cameron himself started off working for downmarket Carlton TV, courtesy of his future mother-in-law Lady Astor who knew the owner. George Walden's 2008 book *The New Elites: Making a Career Among the Masses* is really worth reading on this theme.

But let's revert to the matter of general causes rather than the human stories of how elites operate.

The competence and honesty of financial, regulatory and policy elites were further damaged by the 2008 financial crash, which also revealed the colossal sense of entitlement of the already rich.

They may competitively contribute to (preferably environmental or Third World) charities at crass tuxedo dinners which are cringe-making to attend, but they also barge along like Mr or Mrs Toad in huge SUVs, cross the skies in private jets, or blithely excavate subterranean cinemas and swimming pools under old townhouses. Incredibly, the equivalent of fifty tower blocks have been dug *under* central London in recent years so rich people can avoid going to public cinemas.

That would be the same London which has become like Ali Baba's cave for the ill-gotten gains of the world's super rich. There are guided tours which highlight specific luxury residences like St George's Tower in Vauxhall, home to people who have systematically looted their own countries' resources but who sustain an entire lackey class in London.

The ensuing tribulations of the Eurozone destroyed the more modest expectations of young people in Greece, Italy and Spain, among whom unemployment rose to 50 or 60 per cent, stimulating left-wing populist parties in two of those cases as well as the international celebrity of Yannis Varoufakis—the idol of many Brexit-supporting politicians.

For sure many people were angry at bankers, who became objects of indiscriminate opprobrium, but the buck stopped at elected politicians. As Markus Wagner shows in one of the few decent studies of politicised anger, this was mainly directed at national politicians (and then the EU) who they thought were contractually obliged to protect them from reckless cowboys in the City, for whom austerity was for other people whose taxes also funded colossal bank bailouts. The collapse of RBS worked out at £8,500 for each Scot, and the bailout was equivalent to £740 per head of the whole British population. By 2013 this stake had lost half its value.

Finally, we must address globalisation and its multiple discontents. Technologies controlled by a global plutocracy provided the illusion of intense community among the aggrieved, while reducing complex issues to 140 characters, a thumbs up or down, and an emoji. Outrage became infinite within hermetic silos of the likeminded in media which are supposed to broaden minds but which in user reality are as imprisoned within the nation state as anything else since only a small percentage of searches venture abroad.

Globalisation meant the erosion of the familiar, and feelings of loss of control over cultural identity, not to mention manufacturing jobs lost to outsourcing. The 2015 migration crisis enabled academic sects like Ukip or the AfD—where professors had initially obsessed about currency and sovereignty—to metamorphose into mass parties primarily focused on curtailing migration. Major terror attacks in Paris and Brussels between November 2015 and March 2016 ensured facile real-time elision of migrants and terrorists.

The effects in Britain were reflected in the 2016 referendum. Ironically, it was the British who were most in favour of the European Single Market Act in 1986 which facilitated labour mobility; it was the British who advocated European enlargement (up to and including Turkey) in order to dilute the Franco-German or Carolingian core; and the British who airily refused to impose quotas on economic migration from the new East European accession states after 2004 as they were entitled to do. A hypothetical 10,000 Poles became nearly a million.

Migration was also magnified as an issue in countries which had lost so many young people to the more dynamic economies of western Europe where wages could be five times higher. An exodus of young people, in some cases involving more than a quarter of the population, left older people behind, who felt they were losers, especially after the concurrent arrival in the 1990s of besuited westerners with the know-how to demolish their old industrial economies.

Let's take Thuringia where in 2019 the AfD almost doubled their share of the vote. Since the 1990s, Thuringia has experienced the departure of 445,000 people (leaving 2.1 million behind). Since young women from the service sectors found it easier to move, this left a lot of unattached males, who following the collapse of Communist heavy industry had gone from being heroes of socialist labour to unemployed losers. The only places with a worse gender imbalance than the former DDR are within the Arctic Circle. These Eastern men are very angry.

Now just as antisemitism does not need any Jews to flourish, so anti-migrant racism does not need real migrants, as one can see in the four Visegrad Group countries (Hungary, Poland, the Czech Republic and Slovakia) founded in 1991, which have strenuously resisted the imposition of migrant quotas by the EU, even though regional structural aid is now a larger EU budget head than the entire Common Agricultural Policy. It is 4 per cent of Hungarian GDP.

Some of these countries went from Red to Grey overnight in demographic terms, as young folk left and the grey-heads remained.

As the great Bulgarian scholar Ivan Krastev shows, one might cunningly turn a domestic demographic crisis into a positive advert for authoritarian illiberalism. This requires ideologues.

For years such marginal figures as the French aesthete Renaud Camus or the Swiss Gisele Litman aka Bat Y'eor have been propounding the idea that liberalism (aided by George Soros, who is Jewish of course) is deliberately seeking to *replace* the population of Europe with Third World helots so as to bring about what Litman called 'Eurabia'. The French ideologue Éric Zemmour actually published a book in 2014 called *French Suicide* to dramatize such ideas. It was hugely popular, despite the absurd title with its echoes of Arthur Koestler's 1963 *Suicide of a Nation*, which was about Britain.

In this idiosyncratic reading, liberal Europe becomes the failed past, while the new illiberal authoritarian Europe becomes the future, and an illusion of large-scale migration into Europe substitutes for home-grown demographic collapse.

The Brexit campaign similarly conflated intra-European migration with the threat of 80 million visa-less Turks, without mentioning that in their vision of global Britain's future, the UK would be open to many more non-EU migrants, a theme which was not dramatized on the side of any bus, especially by all those South Asians who have worked their way to the Conservative cabinet.

The failure of national policy-makers to anticipate many manifestations of globalisation exacerbated the neglect into which parts of countries had long fallen, often through deliberate deindustrialisation.

What our Polish friends call Polska B (eastern rural Poland) had its grim analogues in coastal Britain, eastern Germany, the Pas de Calais, to range no further.

Moreover, in what feels familiar from the 1920s and 30s, we have seen a sharp rise in provincial resentment towards major metropolises, except nowadays it is cosmopolitan and liberal Hamburg, London or Paris rather than Red Berlin, Madrid or Vienna. In Britain the gravest charge that populists make is that 'middle class' opponents of Brexit shop at Waitrose rather than at the cheaper Lidl. Personally I'm glad that since I was a boy in the early 1960s, things have improved since the days when olive oil was only available in chemists to use to unblock our ears rather than for salads.

Others like David Goodhart lament the decline of cosy communities of 'somewheres', and the swift passage of our societies from being the equivalent of traditional country houses, where rules were intuited, to the anomie of hotels and hostels, thereby by-passing the home-making stage.

But surely much of this reflects how we live now, including in villages and small towns which are nostalgically idealised beyond recognition, for populism often involves a heavy dose of sentimentalism towards select parts of populations. In reality the fashion industry or CGI animation for the movies contributes far more to UK plc than fishing trawlers. The majority of which are owned by just five high worth families.

You can't have a viable village school if there are fewer children, a post office if people communicate via email or SMS, or village shops if the goods roll in from Amazon's subcontractors.

Families which hardly talk to each other at mealtimes as they scan their Facebook and Instagram pages cannot be expected to chat with neighbours over the garden fence either. Nostalgia for a lost world disguises complex questions about how we have chosen to live in the present, and our lack of resistance to transformative technologies.

Seek out *Innovation and Its Enemies: Why People Resist New Technologies*, a very good book by the late Calistous Juma, a Kenyan historian at Harvard, and then ask yourselves why you would rather pay at an automated till in a supermarket than provide work for sixth formers, the low skilled or the mentally impaired? Is five minutes of human engagement too much when you spend three hours looking at papers on an iPhone, as mine says I do every day?

Now so far, I have mentioned failures on the part of elites and the inchoate anger of ordinary people, something we hear day in, day out in the media. Something rather crucial is missing.

The representative face of our time is not Hitler, however many moustaches you add to Farage's face, or to Merkel's if you are Greek, but rather Howard Beale, a character played by Peter Finch in the 1976 movie *Network*. He certainly looks very angry.

Younger readers may not be familiar with him however.

Fired as a network news anchor man, Beale has a nervous breakdown, shouting from a window 'I'm as mad as hell, and I'm not going to take this anymore!' This proves very resonant. So much so that he is rehired to rant and shout, until his very popular *pensees* affect corporate interests involving Saudi petrodollars, and he is assassinated live on air by a terrorist group which wants the publicity. What seemed amusingly bizarre in 1976 feels strangely unexceptional in 2021. It is not just incredibly prescient about the media, but about globalised corporate capitalism too.

Let's turn to canalised and synthetic anger.

The US Tea Party partly owed its existence to a real-life Howard Beale. This was hedge-fund trader turned broadcaster Rick Santelli, who in 2009 denounced Obama for subsidising the mortgages of what Santelli called 'losers'. It was Santelli who called for a 'Chicago tea party', thereby launching a grassroots movement which would eventually capture a political party.

Its dominant tone was anger, something that is also apparent in many populist parties I have mentioned. An emotion we routinely use to check behaviour we don't like, perhaps Carrie Symons shouting at Al Johnson one night in Camberwell, or which has been effectively channelled in the interests of justice by the likes of Martin Luther King in the 1960s, or the Black Lives Matter movement more recently, has become an all-pervasive mood, but without catharsis, reconciliation or compromise.

Ironically, those most responsible for orchestrating mass anger are themselves members of elites, however successfully they construe themselves as insurgent outsiders.

There is nothing ordinary about Nigel Farage, a former City metals trader turned talk radio star and Europe's first 'Paypal politician', nor about the AfD co-leader Beatrix von Storch, or to accord her due deference Beatrix Amelie Ehrengard Eilike von Storch, Duchess of Oldenburg, a former banker and lawyer turned populist leader.

Not your usual lawyer, since despite being a fundamentalist Christian, Storch suggested that German border guards might be licensed to shoot illegal migrant women and children, though she took out the children—so to speak—in what was not a public apology.

The well-born Matteo Salvini of the Lega also honed his argumentative skills on *Radio Padania Libera*, a theme I want to move onto before I need a libel lawyer or three.

Mass anger has been articulated and shaped by newspaper columnists (some millionaire quondam residents of Florida) whose idea of the common touch is to call taxi drivers 'mate' and their cleaners 'love' as they write the equivalent of an undergraduate essay once a week; and by the shouty talkers of AM and FM radio; and websites whose comment boxes are dominated by people trapped in a perpetual loop of semi-psychotic rage.

The US illustrates where this leads in terms of democratic political culture, and some of it will remind you of what is happening here in Europe. It is worth recounting how the political consequences unfolded.

When music migrated to stereo FM, the cheaper AM band was rescued by interactive talk radio hosts who adapted the chirpy banter of disc jockeys to politics.

Talk radio thrived especially in rural areas, where people spend hours driving alone, as well as among urban night workers and the old and lonely. The advent of mobile phones meant they could easily participate as John or Jill, anonymously that is.

This audience joined an illusory community, hosted by a specially entertaining and forthright friend who articulated and shaped thoughts in an amusing way.

After the elimination of the federal Fairness Doctrine in 1987, US talk radio became a conservative monopoly—by 2007, 91 per cent of thousands of stations owned by a few monopolies could be so described. It is nice work if you can get it, since Sean Hannity's 2008 syndicated radio contract was worth $100 million over five years.

These shows evolved into a toxic brew of entertainment, news and punditry in which expertise on any given issue was too complicated and boring, and in the case of climate science it is actively denigrated by the happily ignorant. That contempt soon extended to judges and civil servants as well as the much-abused mainstream media, as we have seen in Britain too. Academics were a special category of fiend, whether leftist professors or their allegedly snowflake students. There's a whole sub-industry busy denigrating them, and querying the over-expansion of higher education.

Talk radio and shouty television coincided with floods of dark money deployed for political purposes by libertarian billionaires who if they stood for elected office won less than 1 per cent of the vote. Successive changes to electoral finance laws facilitated further changes, notably the 2010 Citizens United Supreme Court ruling which allowed one to donate to a general cause, but one only espoused by specific candidates.

Having already used pseudo-charities to fund ideological outposts inside complicit and needy universities, and thousands of supposedly independent thinktanks, the billionaires turned to creating grassroots movements, a process known as 'astroturfing'.

Various layering subterfuges were employed to conceal where the funding originated, as journalist Jane Mayer shows in her fine book *Dark Money*. This is how 'ordinary' people angry about federal profligacy, abortion or guns came to join lobbyists for the coal, gas and oil industries, in opposing climate change science or environmental regulation. People with modest money themselves could even be made very angry too over inheritance taxes or such niche causes as maintaining the carried interest loophole for hedge-funds. Imagine getting that one on a placard.

The same combination of forces, the billionaires and the talkers, next usurped the essential function of traditional party cabals of the wily and wise in choosing electoral candidates and leaders, while scalping moderates who were dismissed as RINOs or 'Republicans in Name Only'. We have a version of them called BRINOs over here, who are undergoing lustration within the Conservative party.

Being celebrities, the talkers chaired the nomination sessions, while putting their thumbs on the scales on air too. Using ever more sophisticated data technologies, the radical billionaires gerrymandered local voting districts after insinuating their kind of candidate into state government and legislatures. The logical end of this kind of politics is the perpetual campaign which takes priority over serious government, as one can see in both the US and UK, and the manufacture of outrage integral to it. Stability, and our ability to tune out of politics, are forfeited in a climate where instability and noise are omnipresent and entirely calculated. What do you imagine all the lobby shops, thinktanks and political advisers and consultants actually do? Not to mention the online 'engineers of chaos' as Giuliano da Empoli calls them in an eponymous book.

* * *

In 2018 I shared a panel with Frank Fukuyama who had just published a book on the ways in which politics now revolves around identity. Unlike him I am far from convinced that identity politics is here to stay, for pendulums swing back. Voters may weary of the verbally incontinent *'Troll en chef'* in the White House, discovering a newfound respect for civil servants, judges and professional experts, especially if all their lives depend on it. Across the board declines in newspaper sales, to which the shock value of polemicist columnists are like a (cheap) finger in the dyke, holding back the flood of reader indifference and migration.

Since 2015 migration has lost much electoral salience after the EU belatedly took it seriously, sinking to a fifth or sixth order concern in polls. Social inequality could easily move back up the agenda were there to be another major economic crisis in which profits are privatised and losses nationalised as happened after 2008. Boom and bust have assuredly not been abolished, and as we can see on the streets of Santiago, even something as minor as the reaction to a 4 pesos rise in subway fares can result in troops being deployed. Since Chile often boasts that it is Latin America's Switzerland, I would not rule this out in many of our societies.

We urgently need to do a better job of explaining that liberal democracy involves much more than casting a vote every four years, and in defending the buttresses which make our democracies more than Russia or Turkey—incorruptible courts, a free press, the public service ethos, and universities free to discover the causes of things, among them.

All moves to transform representative into perpetual plebiscitary democracy should be sharply rejected, along with attempts to degrade representatives into delegates. One decision blithely taken by David Cameron in 2013 has resulted in Britain becoming a bitterly divided society. Perhaps the most telling statistic is that whereas 21 per cent of people have no party identity, that only applies to 6 per cent in the case of how they line up on Brexit, four years after the referendum on EU membership.

Elites need to be better at listening, an obvious model being President Macron's updated *cahiers des doleances*—to record the grievances of the Yellow Vests, ironically an idea he filched from Poujade. Only when grievances are specified and quantified can anything be done to redress them. Having been impressed by jury service, maybe citizens assemblies are a way to go? Politicians need the courage too to counter the illusion of limitless options and to spell out geopolitical realities about our world, as Chancellor Merkel does every time she returns from China.

Listening will be impossible if entirely anonymous media executives constantly re-engineer bogus polarisation in their quest for ratings and readership. We are drowning in meaningless noise and we need to identify who is responsible for it. Refusing to join this debased circus is worthwhile too and we need to find alternatives to it.

Contrary to free market dogmatists, the state has a role in improving the material well-being of its citizens by regulating the market and redistributing its bounty, just as it played a role in major technological developments through research funding, as the LSE economist Mariana Mazzucato has shown so clearly. But perhaps instead of the mania for more infrastructure there should be more thought about how to knit together people divided by age, geography and wealth, for example through civilian volunteering at age eighteen. After all, many nations were forged by military conscription, the process the American-Romanian historian Eugen Weber called turning peasants into Frenchmen. The state should also ensure that the security interests of the nation are not subordinated to other powers, be they America, Israel, the Gulf Arabs or many others through the nefarious influence of paid lobbyists. A more populist foreign policy might be a more interesting one, though elites will resist it since we sell a lot of arms to the Saudis.

Effectively communicating real priorities matters too. I mean how Industrial Revolution 4.0 is transforming our lives or the climate change emergency which at least a lot of teenagers grasp. But I'll end with a thought about the rage which we read again and again is so integral to populism, for there seems to be a complete failure to address or analyse it.

Conventionally, intractable international or subnational conflicts are resolved through the equivalent of individual psychotherapy. It's always 'good to talk' as the old BT advert had it.

In 2016 some Israeli psychologists and sociologists conducted an experiment on a very hawkish Tel Aviv suburb called Giv'at Shmuel, two thirds of whose 25,000 inhabitants welcomed the epithet of being right of Attila the Hun. It was the time of the knife intifada.

Instead of enjoining people to be more open-minded, the team hired a PR agency to saturate Giv'at Shmuel for a year with martial posters and online ads, with slogans like 'Without war we would never be moral', and depictions of IDF heroes accompanied by Wagner's 'Ride of the Valkyries'.

When after a year the inhabitants were surveyed on their views, the most extreme had become remarkably less belligerent and more tolerant when compared with control suburbs where there was no ad campaign. And the point?

No one wants to be lumped together with permanently enraged cranks as they look into a mirror of their soul. The Twitter CEO Jack Dorsey's decision to ban political advertising and the Tweeter in Chief is a step in the right direction. So too is ITN News's urgent coverage prompted by death and rape threats to women MPs.

Is this what we have become, or want to be?' the host asked. Maybe societies will then decide, having looked in the mirror, that enough is enough, at least with being 'as mad as hell'.

2

RUSSIA AND BRITAIN

This chapter title may evoke those fanciful couplings favoured by literary critics: Shakespeare and Stormzy or Pushkin and Pussy Riot. I remember polite scepticism from Mick Cox when I first broached this topic. I shall try to lower his eyebrow.

I want to discuss some historical and psychological 'issues' involving Britain and Russia. That means imperial Britain and tsarist Russia, but also the Soviet Union which stridently disclaimed being an empire at all. Instead it was a universally-transferable political ideology, good enough for Angolans, Ethiopians or Germans.

I'll begin with a brief outline of how these empires were formed, before focusing on their dissolution. That means touching on the earliest iterations of empire, which often seem the most problematic to the post-imperial polities that resulted.

This also means touching on a revealing synecdoche, namely the commonplace confusion of English and British, something which also still happens in the case of Russian and Soviet.

An example of this confusion was a *Daily Mail* front page in February 2016 which demanded 'WHO WILL SPEAK FOR ENGLAND?' You had to work down the editorial inside to find the qualification 'and, of course, by "England"… we mean the whole of the United Kingdom'. The original front page was dropped from the *Mail's* separate Scottish edition.

We are so used, rightly, to seeing imperialism in terms of dominance, that we often forget that it invariably involved self-denial for the most dominant nationalities involved. Historically obvious asymmetries of scale meant that in both the British and Russian empires, the dominant nationality had to practise self-abnegation towards the subordinate folk, regardless of what was said in private. That is the deeper meaning of the enthusiastic imperialist Rudyard Kipling's paradoxical question: 'And what should they know of England who only of England know?' for in his time England had become the world.

Some have compared loss of empire to phantom limb syndrome. The amputation was relatively protracted and more sanguinary than some imagine in the British case—taking more than a quarter century in the tightest chronologies. The implosion of the former Soviet Union was very rapid, between 1989 and 1991, if we include the abandonment of foreign clients like Ethiopia's Haile Mariam Mengistu or the collapse of an outer empire which reached into Germany.

Both defunct empires exhibit a worrying disregard for historically-core neighbouring states—in particular Ireland and Ukraine—which they continue to view in a quasi-imperial fashion. Luckily instead of armed land-grabs, we have had much casual anti-Irish chauvinism, or calls for the Republic to follow Britain out of the EU, so as to resolve some of the conundrums the 2016 Cameron referendum caused through cavalier lack of knowledge or foresight.

In addition to exploring all that, I'll conclude with some remarks about the enduring temptations of an Anglosphere and Empire 2.0 during the Brexit era, and how this might impact adversely on the European Union, especially if an attenuated 'Great Britain' undergoes a loss of esteem equivalent to Russia in the post-Soviet 1990s. One of the more distinguished heads of the Secret Intelligence Service has said that the unmoored United Kingdom is destined to be a Tier 3 power, below the Tier 2 likes of the EU, India or Russia, and the Tier 1 duo of the US and China. This may require mental adjustments, though I am not optimistic about that in a society which seems to think it is still 1940 or in which, according to a March 2020 YouGov poll, 27 per cent of Britons wished they still had an empire, and 32 per cent were proud of the past one (with the Dutch in first and second places in their answers to the same questions).

This takes us back to post imperial Russia, which nowadays is not lonesome since its alliance with China is quickening. This last vista amounts to the belated realisation of a Eurasian monolith, which LSE director Halford Mackinder (from 1903 that is) could only dream of when he envisaged a giant continental Euro-Asiatic 'Heartland'.

Some people, especially in Eastern Europe but also the FT's Gideon Rachman, fear an opportunistic pariahs' combination resembling that of the Bolsheviks and the Weimar Republic in the era of Rapallo after 1922 should eight months of trade talks with the EU turn sour. I hope this warrants an hour of your time.

* * *

Rivalry with Russia has always occluded what Britain and Russia share by way of historical experience. They have a deep common history as empires on Europe's peripheries, the former by insular necessity across the Atlantic, and then following the American Revolution, in South Asia and Africa. The Russian empire was land-based if we discount the Alaska venture as eccentric. There are still ninety Orthodox parishes in Alaska, a ghostly reminder of a colonial venture the Russians sold to the US for $7.2 million in 1867.

The Russian Empire was assembled by four successive imperial surges, the first big push over the Urals resulting from 'fur fever'. This was akin to gold rushes elsewhere, as the quest for marten and sable pelts took the Russians into Siberia. Muscovy also struck out south-eastwards against the fractious khanates of the Mongol Golden Horde to whom Muscovy's rulers had been tributaries.

Like many kingdoms and empires, the rulers of Russia made extravagant claims. Tsar Ivan IV called himself Khan as well as Tsar, for he ruled many Muslim subjects. The equally Roman-origin double-headed eagle standard faced east and west. Orthodox clerics supplied the useful conceit that Moscow was the

Third Rome, the successor to Byzantine Constantinople which in 1453 fell to the Ottomans. Messianic religion (Protestant in our case) leads me to the briefest summary of English empire.

The first 'English' empire was even more venerable than Muscovy's, except that England was a Norman French colony. Its prized crown and centralised tax yields were inherited in turn by the Angevin dynasty. The ruling class had such classic English names as Dennis, Richard, Roger or William, except that these were all French. The Anglo-Saxon names are tongue-twisters for a modern Brit.

England's gradually Anglicised ruling elites conquered Wales and Ireland and fought the 'French'—first deemed 'aliens' in Magna Carta in 1215 as it happens—in a protracted war which only concluded in 1453. Only the northern half of Scotland escaped their grasp, though Anglo-Norman influence was dominant in the Lowlands. None of this has much to do with nationalism for these aristocratic elites were thoroughly supranational, think Davos man in armour, while the illiterate common folk (meaning 70% of men and 90% of women even as late as 1642) were sub-national in loyalties.

Forced out of France and roiled by the Henrician Reformation, English claims to insular empire were formalised over Wales in 1536 and Ireland in 1542. Conquest was bolstered by assiduous cultivation of myths about 'Great Britain' as more than a geographical expression.

Dynastic union between England and Scotland in 1603 saw the adoption three years later of the Union

Jack flag, with Jack being a corruption of Jacques or James I/VI. You can see Rubens's rendition of the union of the kingdoms on the ceiling of the Banqueting Hall in Whitehall.

The female figure of Britannia with a shield made her appearance on coins in 1665; James Thomson's rousing Rule song was written in 1740. There was one major source of future trouble.

Starting in the Tudor period, English and Scottish settlers were planted in Ireland, a process aggressively accelerated when under Oliver Cromwell 40,000 more were added in the most Gaelicised part of Ireland in northerly Ulster. These New Irish settlers were militantly Protestant, surrounded as they were by people they regarded as barbarous.

Which brings us to Great Britain. In 1707 a bankrupt Scotland was united with England in a customs union and single market with joint defence too, affording the Scots access to trade not just with England, but throughout its American and Caribbean colonies. The Scots lost their parliament but retained distinct institutions like Roman law. Jacobin-inspired radicalism in Ireland was the main driver of the 1801 Act creating the United Kingdom of Great Britain and Ireland. This was eventually modified after partition in 1921 into 'and Northern Ireland' once the Irish Free State had achieved independence, incidentally a conscious option to become poorer but prouder.

Union was fostered by a common governing class (Wellington, Castlereagh and Palmerston were Irish), by a Labour movement whose heartlands were in Wales and Scotland, which reflected economic transformations in which discrete parts of Britain had first-mover advantages.

The Industrial Revolution which was as evident in Cardiff or Glasgow as Manchester and Bolton was one general buy-in to a relatively new British identity; another was membership of a colonial elite which ruled the gigantic jigsaw puzzle of global interests that became the British overseas empire.

Being 124 times the size of the British Isles at its zenith, this offered limitless scope for ambitious or desperate people, for example the relatively better educated Scots. Between 1850 and 1939 a third of colonial governor generals were Scots, with equally heavy representation in trade, finance and the military. Tombs in the huge Necropolis on the hill overlooking Glasgow are a testament to the wealth they derived from empire, even if the people down below in the Gorbals had some of the worst housing in Europe.

Thoroughly confusing English and British, the settler colonies and future white Dominions were simply viewed as England writ large, as if Australia was greater Kent, but this was an England construed not as a mere nation—like Bulgaria, Italy or Poland—but by race, a favourite word of the Victorians.

Race was a literary and historical rather than scientising term for most of the nineteenth century—signifying a providential mandate to spread law and civilisation akin to that avowed by the Romans.

Faltering confidence in empire, especially during the Boer War, and the growth of an assertive Celtic counter-nationalism in Ireland, led some to eagerly adopt a much more expansive supra-identity as Anglo-Saxons, a term used frequently after 1840.

That was the intention behind what Robert Young calls 'the systolic rhythm' of Oxford's Rhodes scholars, the elite within an elite race that also spanned the US of course. 'Through America, England speaks to the world', as the liberal Charles Dilke optimistically put it.

* * *

Though for a century Britain was the largest empire the world has seen—imperial Rome could have fitted snugly within modern Canada—the Tsarist Russian empire was much larger and persisted for a longer period, even though much of it was sparsely populated.

What you might call the logic of the imperial game was just as evident. Siberia doubled up as a land of opportunity and a place to dump convicts, California crossed with Australia so to speak. Given the flat and open-ended geography of Russia, expansion was driven by the need to fill potential vacuums before other powers did so, as the British found too in Africa, or Afghanistan, where they played a 'great game' with their Russian counterparts.

Deployment of the 'samovar and the scimitar' (or schmoozing and killing) took the Russian empire into the Caucasus, where considerable violence was used to repress Circassian and Chechen clans, and subsequently into Central Asia, where generals like Mikhail Skobelev had a brisk view of the natural order of things: 'I hold it a principle that in Asia the duration of peace is in direct proportion to the slaughter you inflict on your enemy. Strike hard and keep striking till resistance fails; then form ranks, cease slaughter, and be kind and humane to the prostrate enemy'.

Skobelev differed little from the contemporary British colonial administrator Lord Lugard who in 1890 said: 'the native looks on it as a sacrilege to touch a Sahib (the Arabic and Punjabi term for 'Master'), and also expects little short of death from the Sahib if he should try conclusions. To this prestige the white man owes his ascendancy, and it must at any price be maintained, just as one would with a brute beast'.

By the late nineteenth century, the Tsarist empire extended to Vladivostok (Ruler of the East) on the Pacific. It took Anton Chekhov three months to venture that far on a muddy road; his successors could reach it much more quickly by the single track Trans-Siberian railway which was finished in 1903.

Although the British are convinced of their own superiority in these things, in some comparisons the Russians appear to hold the advantage. The highest echelons of the Tsarist court, bureaucracy and military abounded with foreigners, notably Baltic German aristocrats, including some 38% of the total in the case of the top civil service roles between 1700–1917. Their resented ubiquity would be among the drivers of both Pan-Slavism and Russian nationalism.

Nothing in the British empire was akin to arrangements in Russia whereby Animist, Buddhist or Muslim aristocrats could possess Christian serfs, a slightly improved form of slavery. When we look west rather than east, for Russia achieved suzerainty over Finland and Poland too, there is no British analogue to the mock Russian prayer: 'Oh Tsar, bestow upon our own people what you have already granted the Poles and Finns'. And finally, half of the deputies in the first Russian Duma in 1905 were not ethnic Russians, something inconceivable at Westminster despite the Irish and Scots MPs represented there, who were not natives of course.

Before and after the First World War both the British and Russian empires had to deal with a new climate in which even the smallest peoples strove to realise their right to national self-determination. In Russia's case that coincided with Revolution.

The Bolshevik Revolution was an avowedly anti-imperial project, but the Soviet Union, as constituted in 1923, included a Russian Republic which comprised 90 per cent of its territory and 72 per cent of the population, while by 1927 65 per cent of Communist Party members were Russians.

But though most all-Union agencies, from Gosplan via the NKVD to the Red Army had their headquarters in Moscow, Russia paradoxically did not have a national capital, and the Russian Republic had no Communist Party until 1990 by which time it was a different beast.

For Russia was subordinated to both the world-transforming mission of the Bolsheviks and, within Soviet borders, to the requirements of federalism and indigenisation which resulted in at first eight major union republics and myriad autonomous regions for even the smallest nationalities.

As Bukharin put it: 'As the former Great Power nation, we Russians should indulge the nationalist aspirations of the non-Russians and place ourselves in an unequal position, in the sense of making still greater concessions to the national current. Only by such a policy, when we place ourselves artificially in a position lower in comparison with others, only by such a price can we purchase for ourselves the trust of the formerly oppressed nations.'

The effect has often been compared to a communal apartment, in which every other nationality had its own room, but not the sovereignty which came from Russian occupation of the hallways, kitchen and bathroom, but who had no dedicated room of their own.

Arguably, the only time this Red Empire operated as an emotional and functional whole was during The Great Patriotic War, though one suspects Balts, Chechens, Crimean Tatars and Volga Germans would not agree, not to speak of Ukrainians whose homeland was turned into a charnel house, as Timothy Snyder has powerfully argued.

In the decades after the war, indigenisation in the non-Russian republics meant the dominance of a hybridised nomenklatura which discriminated against Russians who from the 1970s onwards began reverse migration back into the Russian Republic. Many there began to agree with Solzhenitsyn's 1974 'Letter to the Soviet Authorities' which deprecated the dominance of imperial over national interests, with the Russians drawing the short straw. As the Soviet Union spectacularly fell short of the goal of achieving Communism by 1980, and the stagnation of the Brezhnev years set in like dry rot, so some Russians turned to their own heritage.

According to Geoffrey Hosking that meant civic groups dedicated to rescuing churches and monuments from ruination, or environmentalists concerned with the fate of Lake Baikal and the stone pine forests of Siberia. Intellectuals began to interest themselves in a non-Marxist Russian tradition, above all Dostoevsky, from whom they derived the idea of a Russian 'soul' so capacious that it could include humanity as a whole.

But regime attempts to instrumentalise Russian nationalism in the service of the Soviet Union could not compete with Russian demands for democracy and sovereignty, whose populist tribune Boris Yeltsin became Russia's first democratically elected president in June 1991, barging aside Gorbachev who had sought to retain the Soviet carapace.

* * *

I want to turn to the mechanics of imperial retreat, a process which took two decades in the British case—excluding the 1997 retrocession of Hong Kong—compared with a couple of years for the Soviet Union to dissolve.

The British empire collapsed under the strains of the Second World War, as the cost of defending empire proved too much for Britain to bear. A major loss of face occurred in East and South Asia after the Singapore garrison surrendered in 1942 to Japanese armies which propagated 'Asia for the Asians' in the European colonies they conquered. Even before the war was won, John Maynard Keynes warned: 'We cannot police half the world at our own expense when we have already gone into pawn to the other half'.

The main pawnbrokers were the anti-imperialist Americans, though after the onset of the global Cold War, Rooseveltian contempt for colonialism was tempered by the need to keep European colonial powers in the global business of containing Communism. This is one theme of my book *Small Wars, Faraway Places*.

Who was really in charge was made clear during the 1956 Suez Crisis when Eisenhower pulled the plug on sterling and the Soviets threatened to drop nuclear bombs on London. Although like the Belgians, Dutch and French, the British fought bloody counter-insurgency campaigns in Malaya and Kenya, they maintained that they had an orderly design for departure from their colonies.

Power would be sedately relinquished to indigenous moderate nationalists, like Banda or Kenyatta, who would re-join a partnership of equals called the Commonwealth as a beacon of multi-racial felicity. As in the case of an earlier Great Britain, the biggest buy-in to a Commonwealth was by the monarchy.

The reality included botched federalist schemes, like the 1953–62 Central African Federation and the serial atrocities which came to light from the suppression of the Mau Mau insurgency in Kenya.

The Commonwealth was also riven with internal disputes between India and Pakistan, many stemming from panicky Partition, and over apartheid South Africa which Britain helped arm. Chronic financial strains led to the retreat from East of Suez by Wilson's Labour government in 1968, though the British elites retain their close relationship with the falcons, horses and deference-based despotisms of the Gulf.

47

Loss of empire in turn raised questions of national identity, notably among outsider observers. In 1962 Dean Acheson told West Pointers: 'The (British) attempt to play a separate role—that is a role apart from Europe, a role based on a "special relationship" with the US, a role based on being head of "a Commonwealth" which has no political structure, or unity or strength...this role is about to be played out. Great Britain attempting to work alone and to be a broker between the US and Russia, has seemed to conduct a policy as weak as its military power.' Famously he added 'Britain has lost an empire and not yet found a role', to which an angry Harold Wilson replied that Acheson had lost a State Department without finding a role either.

Thanks to the golden afterglow of victory in 1945, and the delusion of playing sophisticated Greeks to crass American Romans, the British tended to regard immersion in Europe as an either/or option, whereas their no less imperial European partners—Belgium, France, the Netherlands among them—found membership of the EEC less fraught, and in the second case easy to combine with a lingering quasi-imperial mission still going strong in the Sahel and elsewhere. Although the issue of Europe has been the Bermuda Triangle for so many Conservative prime ministers, one should not forget that Labour were usually the chief nay-sayers.

I owe the following joke to Vernon Bogdanor. In 1967 an ailing Clement Attlee made his final speech to a Labour committee opposed to Britain joining the Community. He rose to his feet: 'The Common Market. The so-called Common Market of six nations. Know them all well. Very recently this country spent a great deal of blood and treasure rescuing four of 'em from the other two'. He then sat down. In 1983 Michael Foot's Labour party ran on a manifesto urging withdrawal from the EEC without a referendum. The spirits of this lived on in Jeremy Corbyn of course too.

On the third attempt, Britain had joined the Common Market in 1973 while hedging its bets through the two other circles of influence, namely the Commonwealth and relations with the US which were so tight that de Gaulle had twice repulsed Britain as an Anglo-Saxon 'Trojan Horse'. Late EEC membership meant an inability to shape the community's creation.

Swathes of the Tory Right were unhappy too, for the ultimate horror for the British imperial ruling class was that Britain 'would become a sort of poor man's Sweden', as a Governor of Aden put it in 1963. Speaking of Scandinavia, you will recall the Danish politician who after the 2016 Brexit vote remarked: 'There are two kinds of European nations…there are small nations and there are countries that have not yet realised they are small nations'. That continues to be Britain's problem as it off-ramps from the multi-decennial diversion into Europe, perhaps in vain hopes of a special relationship which in reality the US only has with Israel. The election of Joe Biden in November 2020 may reinforce that trend.

* * *

The speed with which the Soviet Union collapsed in 1991 can be grasped by something that happened to Dmitri Trenin, a Russian foreign policy expert, at

Shanghai airport in 2001. A Chinese airline assistant was perplexed by his passport still emblazoned with a hammer and sickle encircling the globe. She sought higher assistance. That authority explained: 'Sorry, the lady is too young to remember the Soviet Union'.

The Soviet vanishing was speedy. It commenced first in the outer empire, with Lithuania the first republic to secede in March 1990, before the attritional struggle between Gorbachev and Yeltsin resulted in the Minsk declaration that 'the USSR, as a subject of international law and a geopolitical reality, has ceased to exist'.

The LSE's former Russia expert Dominic Lieven has invited us to imagine something similar happening to Britain during its imperial high summer in the 1930s, for the analogy would be anachronistic for the 1990s.

Not only would the whole overseas empire have to break away in one fell swoop, but Scotland and Wales would secede, if one imagines them as akin to Ukraine and Belarus, in other words places which many obtuse English people, like obtuse Russians, do not regard as independent countries at all. Both the monarchy and parliamentary government would be overthrown too, not forgetting an economic collapse worse than the Depression and in which oligarch crooks and gangsters thrived. By 1998 35% of the Russian population were living below the poverty line.

But compared with the disintegration of western European empires, like those of the British, Dutch, French, and Portuguese, Russia's experience was relatively bloodless, if one excepts the thirteen Lithuanians shot dead by Russian troops in January 1991, two wars fought domestically in Chechnya, and inter-ethnic conflicts in independent Armenia, Azerbaijan and Georgia.

The British fought dirty wars in Malaya and Kenya, as well as leaving sanguinary chaos in India and Palestine, while France's attempt to crush the independence movement in Algeria—technically part of the metropolis—resulted in a million dead. Twenty-five million ethnic Russians may have been marooned in the fourteen independent successor states, but excepting Ukraine since 2014, these have not occasioned the troubles associated with the white settlers in Algeria, Rhodesia, South Africa or Protestants in Northern Ireland, the last still being highly fragile of course.

* * *

Loss of empire is partly a psychological affair, as we in Britain know only too well, especially if the once dominant element—be they English or Russian—finds themselves stripped of imperial purpose. Since empire is often a form of disguised outdoor relief for the upper classes—think of the private school fees for diplomats and generals—it is unsurprising that the adjustment process is most difficult there. There was also Colonel Vladimir Putin, watching these events in Dresden, who regarded the collapse of the Soviet Union as 'the greatest geopolitical catastrophe of the twentieth century' though he did not lament Communism and meant the suffering which the Russians underwent in its aftermath.

Both nations are fitfully engaged in rearranging their national identities, something only tangentially related to the profession of writing History.

President Putin is probably the world leader most versed in history, as well as being an exponent of the applied or useful version of it, including manipulating it. Though he thinks Russia's history and his own destiny are synonymous, we should emphasise that he is no more representative of 147 million people than Boris Johnson is of 65 million. I mean the Johnson who once wrote of Africa, currently object of British solicitations, 'The problem is not that we were once in charge, but that we are not in charge any longer'.

Putin has been constructing a Russian identity, from what one might call an historical property box updated for the post-modern age.

Actually, it is not exclusively Russian in an ethnic sense since he has also raided a stream of Eurasian thought, that thrived among exiled White counts become taxi drivers in 1930s Paris. This involves what one might call rediscovering one's inner Mongol heritage, a subject dealt with in a fine book by the *FT's* Charles Clover. Eurasianism suits a Russian leadership which feels antagonistic to the European Union's empire of virtue, even if the fruits of such a Eurasian customs union have been extremely modest, compared with the galloping embrace of Xi Jinping and China through mega gas deals and joint military exercises.

Putin has obliged Gazprom to subsidise a series of 'Russia—My History' exhibitions, the brainchild of his Orthodox confessor, for smells and bells religiosity is part of his mindset too. This is part of a much larger drive for an official history.

There is little serviceable in the October Revolution, certainly not malign state destroyers like Lenin and

Trotsky or the weakling Tsar, though some of the fiercer White Civil War generals like Anton Denikin and Alexander Kolchak have attracted Putin's admiration.

The murderous Stalin cannot be admired, except where he becomes indistinguishable from the almost sacred Great Patriotic War. Quite rightly since every Russian family was touched by its horrors, including the President's own.

Much needs to be overlooked, notably the secret annexationist clauses in the 'strategically-necessary' 1939 Ribbentrop-Molotov Pact, or colossal intelligence failures in 1941. This is revealing since Putin has repeatedly dubbed the forcible expansion of Russian power across eastern Europe a mistake according to Robert Service, his latest biographer.

Putin's biggest hero is Peter Stolypin, the conservative reformer, assassinated in 1911, who tried to transform Russia through non-revolutionary means. Putin frequently paraphrases Stolypin's retort to liberals in the Duma: 'You gentlemen are in need of great upheavals; we are in need of a Great Russia'.

But Putin also admires the state building autocrats Peter the Great, Alexander II, and above all Alexander III (1881–94).

In November 2017 Putin visited Crimea to unveil a huge bronze of Alexander III, the eighth of its kind, whose appeal may be summed up in the statement: 'We can have no policy that is not purely Russian and national'. That seems to mean creating and managing hybrid conflicts while deflecting the West with various kinds of subversion and re-engaging in the Middle East and Africa. Apparently these pyrotechnics are much easier than diversifying the Russian economy from hydrocarbons, the major failure of twenty years in power, not to mention stagnant demographics and widespread poverty. Instead he is wrestling with what Russians call 'Problem-24'—his own bid to become a backseat driver like Deng Xiaoping or the Kazakh Nursultan Nazarbayev. Putin's current manoeuvring involves identifying himself with stability maintenance, so that the 67 year old President can remain such until 2036 when he will be 84.

* * *

England's post-imperial neurosis is of a different kind, for we are not a large country like Russia. The Blair government's resort to devolution in 1998, to head-off demands for Scottish independence, which then had to be replicated in Wales and Northern Ireland, left the English feeling hard done by. Given that they themselves rejected English devolution—or rather reduced it to a dessicated parliamentary mechanism called EVEL (English votes for English laws)—this took the form of rising resentment towards what they dubbed the totalitarian regime in Brussels. Some clever Brexiters identified with the Irish Free State's wars to liberate itself from Great Britain or with the liberal revolutions across Europe in 1848.

Sixty-two per cent of Scots and 56 per cent of people in Northern Ireland voted to Remain in the EU, while a majority in England and Wales opted to Leave. This marked divergence (we'll omit 'London without England'

and other major cities and university towns) has given a filip to Scottish demands for a fresh independence referendum and for a border poll to unify Ireland as mandated in the international Good Friday Agreement.

In Scotland's case this was because the difficulty of re-joining the EU as a new Scandi-style state because of Belgian or Spanish objections was heavily propagated by the unionist side before the 2014 referendum. A lower price of oil, a high fiscal deficit, and therefore the conundrum of what currency to adopt have not vanished in the interim. The English might want a say too, and polls of *English* Brexit opinion show little enthusiasm for the 'precious Union'.

I will substitute a single personal anecdote for the mountains of analysis about the English and Brexit. In 2009, an eminent former newspaper editor and his wife invited me to see Jeb Butterworth's neo-ruralist play *Jerusalem*. It is about a cussed lord of misrule facing eviction, whose caravan in a Wiltshire woods becomes a mecca for all kinds of people discontented with sundry things about modern bureaucratised life, including not being legally allowed to take drugs.

I was less interested in the play than the audience. Ten minutes in, my friend's wife whispered 'I don't think I am going to like this' while her husband's face certified that this was not the Wiltshire countryside they know and love. It was downhill all the way after that.

But at the end the massed Wiltshire posh persons who had block-booked the row in front and knew our hosts, rose shouting 'Bravo'. I wish I had remembered that mésalliance of the rich and disenfranchised when I was asked to predict the referendum result in 2016, for affluent Dorset, Hampshire or Wiltshire were just as pro-Leave as the left-behinds on the coasts or in the post-industrial North. Many are also conventionally patriotic too, indeed a map of recruitment to the armed forces would have been useful to the Labour party.

With withdrawal a done deal, and the implementation period meaning nothing more than stasis, future relationships are the next arduous phase of a divorce, which according to Bloomberg has cost the UK $175 billion so far.

Brexit has revived if not ideas of an Empire 2.0, for India might have something to say about that, then certainly a yearning for either a regression to the buccaneering England of yore, or an 'Anglosphere' based on more or less tenuous ethnic and commercial ties with the US, the former White Dominions, and India.

The 1870 painting by Millais called the 'Boyhood of Raleigh' captures the adventuring side of things, an era before piracy was internationally repressed. Then there are visions of a Global Britain, based on the supposed ties of kith and kin, and/or Edwardian efforts to combine imperial tariff preference (protectionism) with domestic social reform.

These are almost entirely elite ideological concerns, the progeny of clever young men and women who write newspaper columns and short books, or work in think-tanks paid for by Brexit-supporting billionaires. *Ideas for Sale*, as Daniel Drezner dubs this.

In reality, as the economist Adam Posen points out, trade is largely a matter of gravity. Compared with a 450 million strong market on Britain's doorstep, Britain's trade with such small and distant economies as Australia or New Zealand is marginal, with Ireland alone accounting for more UK trade than the BRICS bloc combined too. Divergence is also much harder to achieve than convergence, as trade experts say.

Here I rely on the former UK trade envoy Sir Ivan Rogers among others. One can devise fancy acronyms like CANZUK, or add as many meaningless pluses to Canada, Norway and so on as you like, but the likely result is probably some version of the rolling patched up arrangements the EU27 have with Switzerland, after instant populist acrimony over the emotional issue of fish, a mere 0.12% of UK GDP.

As for a US trade deal, if NAFTA 1.25 or UMSCA is a reliable guide, Trump or his successors may insert endless poison pills as to what we cannot do with China, or have to do with NATO in the Middle East, with 'control' resembling something akin to becoming Airstrip One to the US's Oceania. Should Brexit upset the Good Friday agreement, 40 million Irish-heritage Americans and their powerful representatives in Congress might cut up rough too. Before I forget, in order to hold back China and the EU, Trump sought busily to wreck the WTO, which is the no fuss alternative which 'no dealers' think the UK can fall back on.

* * *

I want to conclude with how these two post-imperial states relate in the present. The relationship is not just chilly, it is more like deep frozen, as Johnson reminded

Putin with a curt wigging in Berlin. I bet a shiver of fright went up Putin's spine. Foreign policy supremos enjoin us to 'manage' this relationship, a euphemism for not having a clue what to do. I need to go back to a bit of History here.

Russophobia is a deep-seated fact of British history, as shown in a good book by John Gleason. It reflects the two empire's different political trajectories as constitutional monarchies and autocracies, and strategic competition first at the Turkish Straits and then in Afghanistan and Central Asia. British liberals, if not British Tories, were great adopters of plucky little peoples, from the Circassians, Chechens and Poles down to the Afghan Mujahadeen, for this country is addicted to globalised moralising even as it undergoes a nervous breakdown. Even the most privileged members of society seem to be abandoning ship for the normality of California.

After the failure to stymie the Bolsheviks, Britain joined a wider struggle against Comintern subversion, only paused for enthusiasm for the Red Army from 1941–45. Then it was back to the subversion again, the world of Burgess, Philby and MacLean.

Nowadays, the doings of spies seem to dominate the relationship. In 2012 the FSB made much of a mystery fake rock discovered six years earlier in a Moscow park, which SIS was using—they alleged—to communicate with pro-democracy NGOs, which Putin promptly banned. The 2006 Litvinenko and 2018 Skripal affairs are simply the most egregious examples of murderous Russian operations on British soil, to which one should add cyber interference in democratic politics and the extraordinary latitude extended to Russian oligarchs as media owners or donors to major political parties.

This tantalises newspapers, in a way that the informed verdicts of George Schulz and Eduard Shevardnadzhe in the 1980s on the CIA and KGB do not, namely that the spies were utterly useless at analysis and prediction, surely the bit of their job which actually matters to their masters.

But what if Britain and Russia were to find a common cause in future? Gideon Rachman senses trouble ahead from the two bad boy neighbours of a strong and prosperous European Union.

Britain and Russia do not share many values, but as Rachman reminds us 'there are also emotions and strategic interests involved'.

Russia regards the EU as almost as much of a threat as the US or NATO, with the added twist that the EU is the alleged source of the 'Gayropa' moral turpitude of Conchita Wurst that Putin deplores.

What might happen were Britain to suddenly undergo the fate of the Soviet Union, together with an analogous economic shock or even the silent tyre-like hiss of deflated national influence should there be a no deal Brexit?

As Rachman writes, 'English nationalists would undoubtedly see the EU as complicit in such malign events: some critics already accuse Brussels of manufacturing artificial problems on the Irish border, unreasonably delaying a free trade deal and encouraging Scottish independence'. To which one should add tabloid outrage about the EU fostering a pro-EU fifth column, for in their eyes an undeclared war is raging between us and our nearest neighbours and partners. Should there be no deal then such antagonism might grow, or rather, could easily be manufactured, especially if Biden snubs the UK in favour of the EU.

The fear is not that Johnson would combine with Putin against the EU, least of all in a kind of war against liberal values, though many Brexit advocates and sup-porters hugely admire every advance by Orban, Salvini and most kinds of fascist. But an angry 'Engerland' might act like Rossiya, by becoming a perpetual nui-sance, vis à vis the club it has flounced out of. That would surely suit President Putin very well.

3

A JOURNEY THROUGH HISTORY,
POPULISM AND NATIONALISM

An involuntary mental lapse must have led me to include the word 'journey' in this chapter since I spend much time groaning when television presenters invite viewers to go on one. Many people are sceptical as to why Jeremy Paxman should guide us through the Victorian era and actor Joanna Lumley through almost everything else. Most of the journeys seem highly familiar, like a dog must experience on a morning walk: 'Oh there's young Buffy or old Jasper', I imagine.

We have entire television channels dedicated to *Yesterday*, with an endless diet of Romans, Vikings and especially World War Two; the latter possibly for the edification of male war-porn addicts returned from the pub or the kind of Tory MP who writes 1940 on cheques. Add in more programmes of the 'gee whizz did you know how to use a long bow or machinegun' variety—or the startling revelation that ancient Romans had lots of sex—and you have most of History on television, excepting such masterpieces as Ken Burn's series on Vietnam of course. It's fair to say that anything involving ideas, beliefs and values gets the short straw or is left to radio.

I had a go presenting a television programme in 2005. I remember beginning one day, just before sunrise, perched in a boat on a lake in the Vendée (we were doing a section on Jacobin mass drownings called *noyades*). It was freezing cold. I said my lines to the camera team sitting in a parallel boat as we all sped off as the sun rose. Any relief that I got three lines right on the first take was dispelled when the director thought it might be aesthetically pleasing to have geese taking off in the background. All enthusiasm for future television work vanished by the ninth take when some geese took flight.

Viewed in a wider perspective, not all history talk is either good or harmless.

Consider an election poster in Thuringia, a small German state which was once in the DDR, and where in 1930 Wilhelm Frick became the first elected Nazi minister in a state government. After elections in October 2019, no party in Thuringia gained a workable majority, though the far-left Die Linke gained the largest share of the vote. Its state premier was therefore in trouble if he could not assemble a new coalition.

Until now, Germany's mainstream parties have used a cordon sanitaire to prevent the far right Alternative für Deutschland—the largest opposition party in the Bundestag—from assuming regional power, or even being involved in supporting anyone else who tries.

This was doubly the case in Thuringia where the local AfD leader Björn Höcke can be legally described as a fascist, for a German court has ruled that this is so. He leads an extreme inner-party caucus called The Wing which the Bundesamt für Verfassungsschutz has put under investigation. Höcke punctuates his fiery speeches with phrases directly lifted from the Nazi lexicon, and openly regrets Germany's post-war 'culture of shame' meaning too many public memorials to the Holocaust, something I will revert to later. He's a former History teacher by the way.

In February 2020, the Thuringian AfD suddenly switched its support from its own candidate to a liberal called Thomas Emmerich who duly became premier, despite his party securing only seventy-three more votes than the threshold designed to exclude small parties from parliaments.

Emmerich's election poster is the point of what may already be too much detail for such an audience.

The caption says: 'Finally a skinhead who paid attention in history classes', for Mr Emmerich has a shaven head and skinheads tend to be ubiquitous on the far-right.

Since both the local Thuringian conservatives and liberals had defied their party leaderships to also support Kemmerich, he was defenestrated within two hours, in a political crisis which also resulted in the resignation of Annegret Kramp-Karrenbauer, the CDU's lacklustre leader, who only the previous month sat on a LSE stage with much respectful fanfare. AKK's fall in turn brought pressure on Mutti Merkel herself to resign the Chancellorship long before the next general election.

As these events suggest, the red line around the AfD just about held, though there are certainly many German conservatives—ironically enough organised as the 4,000 strong Values Union—who want the CDU to cooperate with the AfD to hoover up the votes of small town, carnivorous, diesel car-drivers, angry about the pervasive greenery of Germany's liberal metropolitan elites. That theme was the subject of my first Engelsberg lecture.

Now, I want to develop the historical component of populism, sometimes in contexts where you might imagine it inapposite.

Several regimes in contemporary Europe are making purposive interventions in History, so as to unify their populations, or to divide them into rooted patriots wedded to myths versus elite cosmopolitan subversives.

The latter would probably include most historians, whose activities the Cambridge historian Jack Plumb once compared to woodworm, silently munching the timbers of historical myth, stripping out the fantastical elements which came naturally to ancient Greeks including Herodotus, the father of History.

History has always been subversive. Herodotus tells a story about the historian and geographer Hecataeus of Miletus (550–476 BCE) whose scepticism he admired. Hecataeus visited an Egyptian temple at Thebes. He boasted that the first of his sixteen ancestors was divine. The Egyptian priests pointed to 345 statues representing generations of their all too mortal predecessors, with no god in sight. Sceptical history was born. Christian providential historians in turn dismissed ancient paganism, only to be subverted themselves when the glories of classical civilisation were rediscovered. The priestly humanist Lorenzo Valla examined the Latin of the so-called

Donation of Constantine, granting the Papacy authority in the West, to prove it was written in the eighth rather than the third century.

But only recently have historians become liable for dismissal or prosecution. It could be worse. In 213 BCE China's First Emperor allegedly buried alive 460 scholars, as historians were known in those times. Later, the founding father of Chinese dynastic history was castrated after he criticised the performance of a particular general beloved by the emperor.

Let's turn from ancient China to Victor Orban's Hungary, where statues move around in the dead of night. Since the Second World War, Budapest's Freedom Square has had an obelisk memorial to the Soviet Red Army.

In 1996 the nearby Martyr's Square acquired a statue of Imre Nagy (with his back turned against the Soviet obelisk), a hero of the 1956 uprising who was hanged for treason after a secret trial.

Rather than remove the Soviet war memorial, for that would have been as consequential as it proved for Estonia, in 2011 Freedom Square acquired a large statue of Ronald Reagan. While that made sense because the US embassy abuts the square and Reagan played a major role in ending the Cold War, in 2013 the Hungarian far right added a bust of Admiral Miklos Horthy in the porch of a Calvinist church.

Horthy was the interwar Hungarian autocrat responsible for a murderous White Terror, following a vicious and sanguinary Red one, as well as a leader deeply complicit from 1938 onwards in introducing antisemitic policies, up to and including deporting 20,000 foreign Jews to their deaths in 1941. Three years later, and after the Germans had occupied Hungary leaving him at the helm as their puppet, 400,000 Hungarian Jews were deported to Auschwitz, where they were murdered too.

This brings us to another statue, allegedly a memorial to the Hungarian Holocaust, in the form of a large German eagle descending on the Archangel Gabriel and with 1944 engraved on a talon.

Hungary's small Jewish community were not consulted in the design of a monument which makes no reference to Jews, and which depicts Hungary as a victim nation rather than one whose elites were anti-Semites who collaborated with Hitler. That is thereby downgraded into a matter of debate rather than verifiable historical fact, which may be the point of the whole exercise. This monument was installed during the night of 20–21 July 2014. On the night of 28 December 2018, the statue of Imre Nagy was duly removed. Even though Orban himself had supported the Nagy statue back in 1996, by 2018 he agreed with those who 'wanted to take back our history and our historical spaces' from the liberal left. We are hearing a lot of that here from the likes of Professor Nigel Biggar among others.

Historical revisionism is also evident at Budapest's House of Terror, which commemorates those who died under the major totalitarian regimes, for there is no room for the authoritarian and fascist ones like Horthy and a dozen or so other little interwar autocrats and dictators. That is probably why only one of its twenty rooms commemorates the Holocaust, while nineteen are dedicated to the crimes of Communism. That 'recalibration' of History suits a Hungarian government which enjoys cordial relations with Israel's right-wing populist leader Bibi Netanyahu, even while employing antisemitic images and tropes to drive George Soros's foundations out of Hungary.

Right wing populist politics is no less immune to the culture of grievance and victimhood of other kinds of identity politics, though tedious right-wing dilation against 'political correctness' does not notice its own version of it where ignorance is a virtue.

Exploitation of historical victimhood is also evident in Poland where the current PiS or Law and Justice President Duda sought to criminalise (with fines and three year terms of imprisonment) anyone who spoke of 'Polish death camps' rather than Nazi German death camps situated in occupied Poland, a state the Nazis had abolished in 1939. Fair enough, though that 'crime' might also encompass Claude Lanzmann's great 1985 epic film *Shoah* or the work of historian Jan Tomasz Gross on the pogrom in Jedwabne in July 1941, where the German security police incited Polish Christian locals to kill their Jewish *Neighbours*, the title of Gross's controversial book.

But Polish victimhood can be taken much further than that.

In October 2017 pious people in Warsaw gathered to see a plaque 'In Memory of the 200,000 Poles Murdered in Warsaw in the German Death Camp KL Warschau'. The camp was allegedly situated in and around a tunnel near Warsaw West station, according to claims made by a retired judge in a book published in 2002. Her claims that the tunnel was used as a gas chamber were undermined by wartime Luftwaffe aerial photography which show pedestrians and carts passing through it over a five year period, while the 'sinister' ventilation arrangements were only installed in the 1970s according to the city's own plans. Eyewitness accounts of black uniformed SS men unloading Poles to be gassed were controverted by the fact they habitually wore grey-green and not black ceremonial dress attire when working.

Why would anyone insist on a municipal extermination camp in a tunnel, when in reality there had been a camp in a former military prison in another Warsaw suburb, where 20,000 Poles of various descriptions did indeed die? The answer is called the 'Polocaust', an attempt to assert parity of suffering, allegedly because Jews have gained too great a market share of sympathy and war-related compensation even as 'they' make Christian Poles complicit in the Holocaust. The malign intent behind the neologism is more evident than in the case of the Ukrainian Holodomor, which etymologically goes back to the 1930s when the terror famine occurred. The Polocaust fiction obviously gains traction from the fact that Polish wartime history includes one major example of a vast crime and cover-up, namely the Soviet NKVD's mass murder of Polish elites at Katyn in 1940, ironically something the Nazis did their best to expose a year later. To deaf ears in the case of Stalin's western allies, who in the British case would duly contrive to import the entire SS-Galician division as coal miners, even as they exported captured Russians who had been pressganged into the Wehrmacht, and who were then mown down as they disembarked in the Soviet Union.

The deliberate cultivation of victimhood, and the self-righteousness accompanying it, are by no means solely European phenomena.

In contemporary China, the official version of history is patrolled by a Communist Party which uses charges of 'historical nihilism'—backed up by law suits, fines and imprisonment—against anyone presuming to disagree. That is why few Chinese scholars have caught the current craze for imperial history—excepting the colonialism of others—for the Qing empire (1636–1912) might be found to have relied as much on conquest as charm in adding 1.4 million square miles to China, namely Tibet, Taiwan or Xinxiang which after all means New Territories or roughly 30 per cent of China's total area.

The stress on Chinese national hurt and victimhood is not recent. As the LSE's William Callahan has shown in a fine book subtitled *The Pessoptimist Nation*, it was a major theme of Republican regimes after 1912, echoing the new calendar and secular religious festivals pioneered in the 1790s by the Jacobins in France. Apart from switching from a lunar to solar calendar, China's Republicans introduced a National Humiliation Day in May 1915, whose stations of the cross were rendered canonical in geography and history textbooks including on maps.

National humiliation meant the violent imposition of extra-territorial jurisdictions by foreign imperialists whether European, American or Japanese from the first

Opium War in 1839 onwards. Although China had actually doubled in size under the Qing empire, the emphasis was on how foreign imperialists had halved it, as maps in the 1930 *Geography of National Humiliation* showed. Although the theme had only been alighted on seventy-three years after that era commenced, humiliation would be further extended into a century of suffering after the war with Japan from 1937–45. This procrustean bed from the early twentieth century explains why it has been easy for the Communist authorities to instrumentalise hurt feelings, though that formulation affords them more agency than they possess.

Strikingly, between 1947 and 1990 no books were published on the theme of China's century of national humiliation, which now had to incorporate such outrages as the Japanese bombing of Chongqing and the atrocities in Nanjing. Instead, Mao insisted on a positive story, based on international class struggle as an antidote to 'narrow nationalism and narrow patriotism', the former the subject of a fine book, *Global Maoism*, by Julia Lovell. Even the Japanese could be accommodated to this epic, with the majority of its workers viewed as victims of the ruling industrial-military clique.

That line continued under Deng Xiaoping, who had himself spent eight years fighting the Japanese as a commissar in the 129th Division, which made him unusual in Party terms since the main war Mao waged was against the rival Kuomintang. Indeed the history of the 1946–50 civil war had been upgraded, while the much longer struggle against the Japanese was downgraded, with Taipei displacing Tokyo in the annals of infamy.

When Deng made his historic visit to Japan in 1978, meeting Emperor Hirohito, the need for his host's capital and technological know-how far outweighed the recent 'unfortunate period' in the more than 2,000 years old Sino-Japanese relationship, an anodyne formula for Chinese people being raped and bayoneted to amuse their tormentors. This all changed after China was rocked by the events of 1989 in Tiananmen Square.

While Marxism-Leninism has proved progressively thin, China's history is deep and long. That makes it selectively serviceable and victimhood is at the heart of it, according to a good book by Zheng Wang. Revealingly, courses on post-1840 history have replaced ones on politics (meaning Marxism-Leninism) at all levels of China's education system, and are mandatory for scientists and engineers too.

The century of national humiliation, culminating in fourteen million Chinese wartime fatalities and 100 million internal refugees, has been turned into innumerable physical sites of memory. It is obviously a case of selective memory for there are none to the half a million peasants who perished in 1938 after the Nationalists elected to breach the Yellow River's dykes, as superbly chronicled by Rana Mitter in his *China's War with Japan*. Gradually the Communist Party is also readmitting the Kuomintang to the official story up to and including token bemedaled nationalist veterans at a military parade in 2015.

In recent decades China has witnessed the proliferation of some 10,000 memorials, notably the open calendar commemorating the 18 September 1931 'Incident' at Mukden which led to the Japanese occupation of Manchuria, and the Memorial Hall for the 300,000 victims of Japanese atrocities in Nanjing after its conquest in December 1937.

Deliberate re-traumatisation is hardly an exclusively Chinese phenomenon, and its effects there are as intergenerationally efficacious as elsewhere. Anger has been a theme I've pursued across these chapters.

It would be too crude to claim that anger is simply being instrumentalised by the Communist Party, to distract from multiple domestic grievances, or that the 'sensitivities' of more than a billion Chinese are being manipulated as a kind of populist adjunct to official foreign policy. Again, I stress that China is not unique in this regard since—to take a pertinent example—during the warlike tensions in the Himalayas with China in the late 1950s and early 60s, prime minister Nehru had to juggle his desires for a peaceful settlement of border disputes with Beijing with the aggrieved sensibilities of India's population as the PLA swept over Indian army positions.

In China, such sensitivities can lead to explosions of popular anger, especially among the young and well-educated, as when the Japanese embassy, restaurants and stores were attacked in 2005 and 2012. History was once again to blame, in the first case because the Japanese education ministry had authorised a controversial and self-serving history textbook which caused outrage throughout Asia. The second wave of protests, in 2012, which saw demonstrations in hundreds of Chinese cities, was connected to Japanese provocations and what Beijing regarded as trickery in the East China Seas island disputes which coincided with the date 18 September in China's memorial calendar.

When allied with the ferocious storms which social media can unleash among willing netizens, such protests can become a double-edged sword, leading to the authorities asserting the need for 'rational patriotism' rather than the hysterical mob variety. As a Tang dynasty proverb has it, 'Water can support a boat, but it can also flip it over'. To that end, the Chinese Ministry of Foreign Affairs felt obliged to operate an online chatroom to engage with angry patriots.

` An authoritarian populist regime, as Wenfang Tang has called it, which can and does play off the core ruling centre allied with the restive people, against corrupt or incompetent local and regional potentates, must above all ensure it does not succumb to it. For there is the danger that protests which archly employ the slogan 'Patriotism is not a crime' can also act as a cover for protests against corruption or misgovernment, in which case what are euphemistically called 'stability maintenance measures' click in.

The Communist Party does not rely on codified patriotic history alone, especially because popular nationalism can and sometimes does run amok. China is an ancient civilisation which has relatively recently achieved nationhood. Quite how old was resolved after Jiang Zemin paid a visit to Egypt in May 1996. After learning that the world of the pharaohs was three millennia old, China became a four thousand years old civilisation almost by the time he got off the plane back in Beijing. It is now five.

Emphasis on the venerability of China's civilisation has several useful functions. Particularly under China's current 'Navigator and Helmsman' Xi Jinping this provides a moral compass in a society undergoing the bewildering pace of change portrayed in Yan Lianke's magic realist *Explosion Chronicles*, his 2017 novel about the transformation (in forty years) of a Hunanese village into a mega city. Though neither would appreciate the comparison, what Xi is attempting is akin to the neo-conservative scholar Gertrude Himmelfarb's attempts to re-moralise Western society with the aid of supposedly Victorian values.

Secondly, as Christopher Coker shows, the 'Civilizational State' means one which simultaneously needs no external instruction or tutelage, even as it advertises itself as a model for a new international order based on Confucian harmony and win-win for all. For a very robust advocacy of the Chinese civilizational model try Zhang Weiwei's *China Wave* published in 2011.

And for sure Weiwei is right in this respect: the Chinese have little to learn from the discordant cultural noise of America, never mind its political dysfunctionality, decrepit infrastructure and ability to smash other societies to pieces while blithely preaching the virtues of mom and apple pie—largely to itself.

But there is something surely amiss were we to transpose Chinese experience onto Europe. Imagine we all spoke Latin dialects and still lived in the Roman Empire, instead of individual nation states. However, the later imperial dynasties had been replaced as recently as 1912 by a succession of republics, culminating (after a civil war) in a victorious socialist state which since the 1980s had licensed cut throat capitalism. The confusion would be hard to cope with. No wonder the likes of Weiwei claim that China has a unique civilizational gene, or maybe it is something in the water? For that is the drift of the immensely popular 2004 environmental-fantasy novel *Wolf Totem*, which makes much of the rival wolf-sheep DNA of Mongols and Han, a form of genetic primordialism which has echoes in both Putin's promotion of a unique Eurasian civilisation and the 'pan-Turanian' madness of parties like Jobbik in Hungary.

Like imaginative literature and opera, since the time of Livy history has played a constitutive role in nation-building, a process well described by the Romanian-American historian Eugen Weber as transforming 'peasants into Frenchmen', the title of his greatest book. The only revealing comparator to the processes Weber describes is how rather thin medieval Christian beliefs were deepened by the Reformation and Counter-Reformation as theological awareness replaced ritual and superstition.

This kind of history developed earliest in the Italian Renaissance city states and isolated or insular cultures like Castile or England, but in the nineteenth century many others caught up—Greeks, Italians, Croats, Serbs and Scots among them. Antiquarians who collected and studied old coins and charters to celebrate local place played an unsung role in this process. The National Historical Museum in Athens, located inside the old Greek parliament building since 1960, began as a collection of artefacts and documents lovingly assembled by the Historical and Ethnological Society of Greece since its inception in 1882. Each European nation had similarly dedicated bands of antiquarians and philologists, whose tireless labours never cease to move, even if they are subject to the condescension of historians who prefer documents to inanimate objects and folk tales.

Professional historians were important to this process, nowhere more so than in Germany, the birthplace of modern historical scholarship if that means critical source analysis and graduate seminars with a PhD at the end. Vast collections of sources were edited and printed. Figures like Droysen and Treitschke helped give Germany a sense of itself as something more than a congeries of small states, though the greatest of them all, Leopold von Ranke, did not share this view of the historian's task.

Ranke was a universal historian who wrote about many subjects, always trying to establish 'how it essentially was' from original documents. History was both a science and moral education—*Wissenschaft und Bildung* if you like—certainly not a handbook for rulers, though King Friedrich Wilhelm IV did summon the old boy for an informal chat once a year, in between public lectures which the nonagenarian delivered to awed audiences who could just make out every twentieth word amidst the geriatric ramblings.

Ranke was Prussia's Historiographer Royal, which brings us jerkily to official history.

Arguably, the greatest book on the causes of the First World War was by the *La Stampa* editor and parliamentarian Luigi Albertini. Most countries have official historians, particularly of foreign policy and intelligence services. They work within carefully defined parameters, particularly in the latter case, and are not given to biting the hands that feed them. So do military historians, though there was some delicious irony involved when a friend of mine, a lieutenant-general who commanded the SAS at every level, found himself (and his history of the Falklands War) in contravention of non-publication rules which he had introduced himself, to cut down the number of dubious memoirs cum thrillers which adorn airport bookstores.

Individual regimental histories have been produced for a long time, but contemporary armed forces engage in 'lessons learning' both through post-mission debriefings but also the academic study of warfare at military academies. Some of this deserves to be treated sceptically since I have read many books on counter-insurgency or COIN warfare which omit the only question that really matters, which is whether outsiders should be in Algeria, Malaya, Vietnam, Afghanistan or Iraq in the first place.

There is a psychological aspect to these involvements of historians with power, which is rarely addressed either. It is always nice to be thought terribly important by those in power, though as it happens that can sometimes not be in a good way either.

During the late 1980s I spent some years researching hundreds of German experts on the anthropology, economy, history, philology etc of Russia and eastern Europe. It is called *Ostforschung* in German, something less neutral than 'area studies' since the (German) East had quasi-mystical meanings. These were not top tier people, as you can see from the fact that they often worked in the institutional forerunners of thinktanks, often a give-away sign of mediocrity and ideological zealotry—or *Ideas for Sale* as the American journalist Daniel Drezner calls a certain type of academic entrepreneurialism.

The *Ostforscher* made themselves very useful to Weimar and Nazi governments which used their work to support revanchist claims against the interwar successor states. By proving a deep German presence in parts of Czechoslovakia, Hungary, Poland or Russia, one could keep contemporary territorial claims 'live' or 'green'. After 1939 these people got their chance to turn ideas into practice once Nazi Germany had embarked on its bid for empire. Evincing zero moral qualms, they busily assisted enforced and large-scale population transfers (*Umvolkung* in Nazi German) and worse, enthusiastically eradicated what they regarded as a Jewish mercantile class from entire economies.

I could easily cite other examples, from outside Europe. Long before the 1994 Rwandan genocide, Hutu Power extremists sought to depict the minority Tutsis as akin to privileged cockroaches. The historian Professor Ferdinand Nahimana is not a household name, but after producing many books and articles, he founded *Radio Television Libre des Milles Collines* which directly incited the genocide, with stridently hateful claims and songs openly calling for mass murder by the Interahamwe militias he was involved in creating. He was jailed for life for hate crimes at the International

Criminal Tribunal for Rwanda, though this was reduced to thirty years on appeal.

History can also be a very public affair, orchestrated to achieve political effects. This can mean commemorating something, or not, for omission can also be revealing. In my second chapter I talked extensively about how this plays out in Putin's Russia, so let's pursue the theme in a different context.

Public commemorations tell us much about how governments and nations wish to see themselves. This is *history* reduced to national *memory*, two things which are dangerously conflated nowadays, for memory is even more slippery than history which at least has a basis in documented facts, though as stories from China's digitised archives show, these can literally vanish too.

The 1938 centenary of the 1838 Afrikaner Great Trek was a hugely important consciousness-building exercise for that people, leaving a monumental trace in the Art Deco buildings of Pretoria their capital.

It speaks to an Afrikaaner sense of victimhood at the hands of the British who had an English-speaking fifth column in the Afrikaaners' midst. Boer suffering at the hands of the British was real enough—tens of thousands of them perished in our concentration camps—which partly explains why so many Afrikaaners sympathised with the Nazis who developed such camps into a higher order of frenzied destruction. This history of the vanquished white tribe (or rather one of two) in turn presented a problem to the post-apartheid government of multiracial South Africa. In 2001 the ruling ANC decided to ignore the centenary of the Boer War as a conflict merely between rival white people, until they were reminded of the tourist revenues they might rake in from those eager to tour old Boer War battlefields.

This raises the interesting issue of consciously forgetting, for some societies have deliberately opted for purposive amnesia when their past is too painful, rejecting a mainly German insistence on memory as national psychotherapy, which has real world consequences too in contemporary defence and foreign policy.

Some people claim that having no historical memory is to make adults equal to children, or people who have undergone a lobotomy. Neurologists know the famous 1950s case of a 27 year old patient known only as NM who underwent a 'bilateral medial temporal lobe resection' which left him unable to remember anything after he was aged sixteen. Worse, his short-term memory went too, which is why day after day NM did the same jigsaws and read the same magazines, as if he had not done so for many days, months and years before. Imagine if entire societies ended up like the unfortunate NM.

But in reality, it is equally possible that a surfeit of memory can make adults childish, as they cling to something much more akin to myth than to the ambiguous complexities which our woodworm historians reveal about the past. 'Humankind cannot bear to much reality' as a great poet said.

Both Germany, which I started with, and Japan, have plenty of people who have had enough of what they regard as national self-abasement, which is why their revisionist history is so contentious among their neighbours. As my second chapter showed, the English/British are not immune to this either, with plenty of people here fed up with hearing about the crimes as distinct from the virtues of Empire, for History like much else in life has become a surrogate law court in which the past is constantly relitigated or used for political effect.

As David Rieff shows in his important *In Praise of Forgetting*, too much remembering can lead to a kind of hubris of the 'we were really, really bad' variety, but also to the familiar *ressentiments* of any victim group, overly insistent on the uniqueness of its suffering. This risks competitive victimhood—a civil war of acronyms—something alive and well in the modern Academy of course. Rieff and others feel that George Santayana's famous dictum 'those who cannot remember the past are condemned to repeat it' could do with a little rest, especially since memory is tending to overwhelm history, memory being little more than politicised history and collective therapy in Rieff's view.

Too much memory is a bad thing, as one can see from how a certain memory of the Confederate losers in America's Civil War has been lovingly tended, for that struggle was assuredly not about columned porticos, honour-bound generals and pretty blondes in capacious frocks on a moonlit evening among the magnolias, but about the right to own fellow humans as slaves. Under Trump the first tendency seems to be flourishing, merged as it is with the so-called Alt Right.

I had a recent experience of public history costing about £55 million. Having written extensively about how history is subject to the shifting dictates of politics, this experience had a certain grim fascination. Not least because in the five years it took to decide how to commemorate the First World War, we had seven secretaries of state, including one who appeared once for fifteen minutes, claiming he felt like a player on a football pitch after eighty-five minutes, and another who did not appear at all.

The Cameron government was keen to commemorate the First World War, not least as they faced a tricky independence referendum in Scotland in 2014, and wanted to emphasise the ties binding the four nations of the Union. What our panel of the great and good did not commemorate was revealing. We omitted the causes of the war, how commanders fought it, and then the question of whether it was a strategic defeat as it had to be refought twenty years later—a point made insistently by a former Chief of the General Staff as it happens. Apart from being alive to every conceivable diplomatic tonal sensitivity, from the Irish to the Turks via the Chinese Labour Corps and Indian Army, our main remit was to ensure that every young person empathised with the lowly Tommy who may have been their ancestor. Fair enough, but I doubt this will be repeated when our descendants reach 2114, by which time AI will have absorbed every single evidentiary trace of the war and rearranged it. Frederick William Maitland once invited us to remember that events in the past were once in the future; it is useful to imagine our future will regard towards what we view as the past too.

And so we come to applied history, the most recent way in which study of the past is being instrumentalised.

Many know Robin Collingwood's famous observation that the historian is like a trained forester, knowledgeable about animal tracks and prints, compared with some oaf blundering through a forest who does not see the lurking tiger. If only politicians had read as many books as all of us. What if Gorbachev had studied de Tocqueville, in the way his *Ancien Regime and the Revolution* is mandatory reading throughout the contemporary Chinese Communist Party, which, by the way, has also produced a boxed DVD set for its cadres on what Gorbachev did wrong.

The trouble though is that any historical advice is likely to be sought from those who already fit a kind of governmental group think, and that politics is a real-time exercise with real consequences and done by grown-ups. Not all voices count equally either, and we can be sure that some professor in the corner will not have the equivalent weight of industrial and foreign governmental lobbyists backed by all the dark arts of PR which will ensure we will never cut ties with the Gulf Arabs or Israelis. Moreover, the range of historical questions asked by applied history seems to have scant space for how health care or prisons were organised in the past. Or indeed how societies react to mass pandemics, like the one which cancelled delivery of this lecture in March 2020.

The only Thucydides Trap is not the one involving Sparta and Athens opportunistically updated to the US and China, but the one set by Thucydides himself when he reduced history from how Herodotus conceived it, to what the great Italian ancient historian Arnoldo Momigliano called the iron tower of political history—including diplomatic history in its most dessicated forms.

This seems an unimaginative understanding of what we can learn from the past, which Thucydides also reduced to the near present. What about how people have sought to resist novel technologies? How did beer and salted herring producers react to the ruination they faced from coffee houses, or dairy farmers to oil-based margarine? Well they said coffee made men impotent while margarine had to be packaged in lurid pink boxes marked with black crosses underlining its 'toxicity'. Surely that history has some bearing on our over-technologically determined lives? Similarly, in societies divided by every kind of public rancour, to the point of undermining democracy itself, shouldn't we be looking at how societies recover from conflicts, or the role of forgiveness, which in this age of angry accusation seems to set the dominant tone?

Doesn't anger, like any human emotion, have a history, a theme I touched on in the chapter above? Here it is a case of the West not knowing best, and it has a bearing on what I suspect will not be elite foreign policy-making for much longer.

Ironically, some of the very best studies of mass anger have been produced by scholars writing about China. They concern the Internet 'Angry Youth' and the 'human flesh eaters' or flash mobs, which first appeared both in China and among the diaspora during the Olympic Torch saga in 2008 when they felt humiliated by the West. While some are patriotic protestors (hence the name 'April Youth' which echoes the 4 May Movement of 1919) others reflect resentment at the corruption, power and wealth of China's 'meritogarchic' elites, or are a non-political way of letting off steam in an over-examined and over-stressed society in which some people are bound to fail, a subject our applied historians might turn to as well as we undergo the revolt of the low achievers and the working poor. Ironically, one conspicuous Chinese failure called Han Han used the Net to broker failure into such success that he was chosen as one of the 100 most successful people in the world by the *New York Times* in 2010. There is surely much Western societies could learn from this in our own populist moment.

Those strike me as far more pertinent questions than endless rehashing of the virtues and vices of appeasement (as if we are stuck in a perpetual Munich in 1938) let alone more 'purposive' applications of the 'lessons of history' which may not be of much contemporary use at all. By all means go down this route, but not in ways which close rather than open minds, or at least flatten them to an eternal near-present, rather than exploring the incredible depth and richness of the human past which has many lessons to guide us with, if one can cut out the deafening surface noise of the time we live in.

4

POPULISTS AND THE PANDEMIC

WILL THIS BE THE END OF THEM?

The final Engelsberg lecture was scheduled for what I will call 'BC' or 'Before COVID-19'. Twelve weeks of lockdown in London during the pandemic prompted these thoughts on how the pandemic will affect many of the people and themes dealt with in my lectures. The fact that the final one had to be delivered via online video shows how this crisis has affected even something so mundane as giving a lecture, though that is the least of our problems given that hundreds of thousands of people around the world have died in this pandemic.

Most of the world's populist leaders have not had a 'good' pandemic crisis, but some may profit if there is a major economic depression on the back of it. That is not quite what happened in the 1920s and 30s, for Mussolini was in power by 1922, though History does not repeat in exactly the same patterns. What in BC (Before Coronavirus) seemed to be populism's ineluctable rise, is likely to mean a much more doubtful future for them as we enter AC (After Coronavirus). It may be useful to begin with a brief tour d'horizon of some of the main players.

The inadequacies of former President Trump's responses to the pandemic are too numerous to chronicle and exacerbated by his preference for loyalists over the competent. In what sane world should his son-in-law Jared Kushner be leading a parallel Coronavirus task force? Dismissing the deadly virus as akin to flu has had tragic consequences, namely a death toll that has far exceeded American fatalities in the Vietnam War—a quarter of a million people and counting. Recommending that people ingest disinfectants or ultra-violet 'lights' left the world incredulous. Trump's sympathetic responses to bearded heavies with firearms invading Democrat-controlled state legislatures to extort a lifting of their lockdowns triggers thoughts of a new Civil War. Joe Biden, the Democrat winner did not even have to leave his Wilmington basement to move ahead of the omnipresent Trump in the polls, winning by a huge margin.

The performance of Trump's fellow strongmen is similarly dismal. The Filipino president Rodrigo Duterte belatedly locked down Luzon's sixty million inhabitants, including in the capital Manila, and then urged the police to shoot dead curfew violators, which at least speaks to a certain consistency in his case. Indian premier Narendra Modi gave 1.3 billion people four hours (before midnight) to prepare for a long curfew. While middle class Indians were flown home, no expense spared, 100 million migrant workers were encouraged to return to their home villages, in dismal scenes which resembled Partition in 1947. Meanwhile, his Hindu nationalist-dominated AYUSH (Ayurveda, Yoga & Naturopathy, Unani, Siddha and Homoeopathy) ministry insisted that homeopathic cures would see off COVID-19 in a country with lamentable health care coverage outside a few states like Kerala.

The strange Brazilian President Jair Bolsonaro was another who insisted that COVID-19 was just 'a meany little flu'. Comments like 'We will die someday' were of little help to those in *favelas* awaiting the grim reaper. He persisted in glad-handing on his casual progress through open air markets, and then brought twenty-three aides—many of whom subsequently tested positive for the virus—on his March visit to President Trump's Mar-a-Lago resort complex.

He sacked Luiz Henrique Mandetta, the orthopaedic paediatrician turned capable health minister, and the most popular politician in the country. The justice minister Sergio Moro then resigned. Moro led the Operation Car Wash corruption investigations which led to the resignation of leading politicians far beyond Brazil itself where the president was impeached in 2016. Moro objected to Bolsonaro's rigging of the appointment of a chief of police, just as two of his sons, Flavio and Carlos, were about to be investigated for corruption. The president has lost support from Brazil's state governors, including his erstwhile supporters, while the military (to whom he panders) are distancing themselves from him too since as elsewhere in Latin America they are stepping in to help during this public health crisis. They are not the same political soldiers who swept dictatorships to power throughout Latin America in the 1970s and 80s. Nowadays peacekeeping and disaster relief keep them busy. Meanwhile, the carefree president took a speed boat to a floating barbeque even as talk swirled of impeachment, which is a serious prospect in Brazil.

This is not a merely a right–left political point. Mexico's left-wing president, Manuel López Obrador, was equally determined to ignore coronavirus, insisting that the best cure was for Mexicans 'to hug' and 'take the family out to a restaurant'. But the real prize for obtuseness goes to Nicaragua's combo of Daniel Ortega and his wife and Vice President Rosario Murillo. She called for mass marches, framed as 'Love in a Time of Coronavirus', in which people donned virus-styled costumes. Worse, children were encouraged to greet disembarking cruise liner passengers, which is akin to asking kids to bathe in a giant petri dish.

In Russia, President Putin's grip on power seems less certain during this crisis, even though Russia has certain built in advantages since its cities are spaced across eleven time zones. He has surrendered dealing with the crisis to capable mayors like Sergey Sobyanin, or to regional and city governors who are often oligarchs in what are often mono economies. The latter have been told to shape up and to open their pocket-books to cover wages. Putin seems bored and disengaged whenever he appears on television to listen to others talking about a pandemic which is especially grave in Moscow. He had to cancel the 75th anniversary 9 May Victory parade which was to be the highlight of his reign, including inauguration of the new cathedral whose architectural 'numerology' reflects the war itself. He postponed then held the referendum to keep him in power until 2036 in one role or another, perhaps as a backseat driver like China's Deng Xiaoping. As oil prices collapse, as a result of a macho contest with the Saudis, Putin will have to decide whether to deploy Russia's reserves to prop up the likes of Rosneft (whose directors just received $600,000 bonuses) or to let the urban middle class fall into penury.

European populist leaders are not having a good crisis either, as we can see in Britain where fanzine focus on Boris Johnson's personal health and a delusional wartime nostalgism cannot mask chronic failures of policy, despite Britain being 'best' at everything. A cabinet chosen for its orthodoxy on Brexit meant that it consisted of second and third-raters whose incompetence is revealed almost daily. Meanwhile, bereft of the oxygen of publicity, Mr Farage cut a lonely figure as he bestrode the beaches of Kent in search of illegal migrants to make a media splash over. He is now essaying a new party 'Reform' to oppose imperfectly executed lockdown requirements. Hungary's illiberal prime minister Viktor Orbán, the darling of the national populist international, has used the crisis for a naked power grab in which he awarded himself five year emergency powers, while not perturbing many European 'conservatives'. This followed years of real curbs on media independence and the licensing of corruption by his big business cronies.

Germany's main opposition party, the Alternative für Deutschland has seen its poll ratings slide, even before a schism loomed between those who wish to appeal to disaffected conservatives and an east German neo-Nazi 'Wing' which is now being monitored by the BvS intelligence agency. Austria's populists were devastated in the recent elections.

In Italy, where the abrasive Matteo Salvini once seemed unstoppable, his Lega's support has fallen by 7%, not least because one of the worst affected regions is Lombardy which the Lega governs. Worse, his colleague Luca Zaia who governs Veneto, has made such a good fist of handling the crisis (the Veneto death toll is a tenth of Lombardy's) that Lega members are openly discussing him replacing Salvini.

By contrast the technocratic prime minister, law professor Giuseppe Conte, is still popular, as is the German chancellor Angela Merkel, a quantum chemist who knows what she is talking about.

Populists have failed in this crisis because their style of politics is maladapted to dealing with something one cannot attach a sinister face to, be it Michel Barnier (though despicably one British popular newspaper tried that by claiming he had infected Johnson) and financier George Soros, or 'migrants' who it transpires often go on to staff our health services.

Trump referred to 'Beijing Biden' in an opportunistic attempt to conflate the Democrat nominee with China, but this did not avail him in the election against the Democrats, who campaigned against an incompetent and polarising incumbent who, in November 2020, lost by a massive majority. Trump's main claim to fame, a booming economy, turned to ashes amidst lengthening lines at foodbanks and for unemployment benefits.

The populists' dismissals of 'experts' sound crass at a time when peoples' lives depend on them; though of course, others inhabit a crazy online ecosystem where 5G masts are blamed for COVID-19 and are being burned down. Their belief in the exercise of unified national willpower sounds hollow and is no substitute for expertise and mastery of detail where there is no margin for error. Though not all national populists are economic libertarians, the latter faction sound callous when they insist on raising lockdowns, even if this means that a lot of old or vulnerable people will die as the second or third wave of the virus erupts.

Some commentators claim that women leaders have been better at dealing with this crisis than men, pointing to Finland's Sanna Marin and New Zealand's Jacinda Ardern. Rather desperately they tack on Queen Elizabeth II. In reality it is not accidental that the countries evincing high levels of competence in dealing with the pandemic include Colombia and Peru or Romania and South Africa, as well as the more familiar Germany, Israel, Singapore, South Korea and Taiwan—and yes, China too—whose leaders have listened to experts, done much testing, enforced lockdowns, and have creatively used technologies to stem the virus's spread. It helps if there has been experience of mass epidemics, as in East Asia or South Africa in the case of AIDS.

It is far too soon to decide what if any long-term political impacts this dreadful crisis will have since it is ongoing.

Optimists claim that now is the moment for liberals to fight back after a decade of being battered by a so-called national populist wave. Enough of the charlatans, entertainers and showmen; seriousness is sexy again. Enough of the snarling nativism which we have seen enough of. This moment has exposed the emptiness of the populists' soundbites and stunts, as well as their nasty habit of blaming outsiders. Even the *Daily Mail* welcomed the return of Romanians to pick vegetables since the lumpen British certainly would not. Liberals might also conceivably benefit from unease that the intrusive state resulting from the virus—in Israel the security agencies are being very helpful with tracking technology hitherto used against terrorists—are a threat to civil liberties of a kind familiar from the surveillance state in China.

Unfortunately, I am in the pessimistic camp though that is not my nature. There is already a rift, alluded to above, in which populist leaders like Trump pit the 'real people who want to get back to work asap' against the 'LameStream Media' who he berates and mocks at his interminable press conferences. This led to his chief medical advisor Dr Anthony Fauci having to have a security detail. He is not giving up on the forces of ignorance which put him in power in 2016 and indeed on 6 January incited them to storm the US Capitol leading to his second impeachment.

Worse, if he grows desperate an already erratic Trump could engineer a military confrontation. The most obvious bet is with Iran, which is already involved in attacks on US bases in Iraq, and an almost daily low-level confrontation with the US Navy in the Gulf. If total pressure from Trump leads Iran to abandon the 2015 JCPOA nuclear deal, restarting a programme it ceased in 2003, then the US might decide to strike. There are also daily tensions in the South China Seas, though Trump needs a trade deal with Beijing to reflate the US economy, while his military know that China's modernised PLA is an entirely different order of opponent in their own backyard than the Iranian mullahs.

Europe's national populists may have had to relinquish the airwaves to steadier voices, but in any protracted economic crisis they will return.

All the advantages of highly specialised economies are already going into reverse as people consume less and supply falls. For the moment there is a fool's paradise as huge sums of money are poured out to mitigate the effects of the crisis on what are after all our tax-payers.

Global travel will be a thing of the past especially as people will need a health certificate as well as a passport and visa and then might face a fortnight in quarantine rather than a holiday or conference. Much of the familiar consumer infrastructure, from shops selling cheap clothes and shoes to bars and restaurants will disappear. 'Decoupling' by shortening global supply chains may lead to something resembling the late Roman Empire in which an imperial economy which centralised glass or tile production in a few factories was replaced by local, hand-to-mouth craftsmanship of an inferior kind. It took a thousand years to get back to the time when even a shed for animals had terracotta tiles on the roof. Unlike after the financial crisis of 2008, there will be no popular patience with further austerity. Any signs that economic inequalities are not being addressed this time will not be so passively received by people who really know the value of their nurses, garbagemen and delivery drivers *vis a vis* bankers and lawyers. No amount of servile stenography for the super-rich by their corrupted newspapers will change that.

The French President Macron has not had a good crisis, with 60 per cent of people regarding him as 'a bad president' even though he was one of the few leaders to admit that he made mistakes. His tardy responses to an outbreak which was evident in neighbouring Italy were only slightly less slow off the mark than the British, and there were similar problems about PPE. His decision to proceed with municipal elections on 15 March looked obtuse, especially as a day later he cancelled the second round and imposed a lockdown on 47 million people. Egregious police violence in some of the banlieues only reinforced what the Yellow Vest protestors experienced earlier, with rubber bullets taking out their eyes.

With France's latest quarterly GDP figures down by almost 6% (the worst since 1949) one would not like to bet on Macron defeating Marine Le Pen when elections are held in 2022. Le Pen initially stumbled by self-isolating even though it transpired she was asymptomatic. She then appeared to welcome Macron's bans on foreign travel and closure of France's borders as a sign he had resiled from liberal globalism.

But she is back on the offensive, blaming a lab in Wuhan for an engineered virus, and mosques for spreading it. She may well use any Depression as a chance to side with the little folk against *les gros*. Expect demands for rent controls or suspensions and swingeing taxes on dividends and the like. Combined with attacks on Muslims, this will put her back on track to attack

Macron as the incarnated representative of the global rich exploiting the *couches populaires*.

We have already noted the steady public deflation of Matteo Salvini, but at the same time the poll ratings of the neo-Fascist Brothers of Italy have sharply risen (almost catching Five Star Movement on the descent) and Giorgia Meloni its leader is the third most popular party leader in the country. Meloni co-founded the Brothers, whose name derives from the Italian national anthem, after Silvio Berlusconi's right-wing coalition imploded in 2012. She was one of his ministers (for Youth) at a time when he wanted pretty faces and included models and the like in the cabinet. The Brothers are the direct descendants of earlier Fascist parties like the MSI (Movimento Soziale Italiano) and indeed Meloni has put several grandchildren and great-grandchildren of Mussolini on her party lists. Meloni's programme includes attacks on migrants and on LGBT rights (she claims to be a staunch Catholic) as well as a Trumpian enthusiasm for low taxes and big infrastructure projects.

While this Sister of Italy won't lead the next right-wing government, she might be a more important member of it than Salvini whose star is on the wane. So far, Meloni (and Salvini) have declined to make common cause against the EU with the wilful leaders of Hungary and Poland. But if the German constitutional court continues to controvert the ECJ and the EU over joint liability bond issues, then Meloni might make common cause with Orban's crusade against the EU's liberal imperialism.

Populists rose to prominence with sneering attacks on global cooperation and 'rule' by experts, civil servants and technocrats. They created the illusion that they are the unstoppable wave of the future. The only prospects for eliminating COVID-19 lie in concerted international cooperation by scientists to find a vaccine. Thankfully several are in production and await delivery. The experts and technocrats have proved their worth in making sense of a threat which most people find terrifying. Punchy slogans are no match for an enemy one cannot see and which does not care what any of us think at all. Attempts to hitch populist parties to anti-lockdown sentiment have failed since libertarians then find themselves in the company of those who think 5G masts cause COVID-19 or that the world is run by a cabal of paedophile Satanists operating from the basement of a Washington DC pizzeria. While this should mark a major turning point where we think about how leaders relate to our societies, the hard times ahead may give these same populists, or their successors, a second wind though in time they too will fail. That is the view of Finland's Timo Soini, cofounder and leader of the True Finns. In 2019 he and his ministerial colleagues left the party to continue in coalition government, but then real responsibility proved too much for him. Like Farage he has become a highly paid speaker, moving from gig to gig. The new head of what are simply called The Finns, Jussi Halla-aho, is far more radical than Soini on Islam and race. When the recession kicks in, Soini claims populism will spring back like a jack-in-the-box. We have been warned, even if the defeat of Trump by Biden definitely has its consoling aspects—and not just for many Americans.